Contents

Cover: The Zulus' struggle for survival—
at Isandhlwana (1879) they defeated the
British
Front endpaper: British troops prepare
to attack an enemy position in the Boers'
own battle for independence
Rear endpaper: The 'Rivonia trial' of 1964,
which effectively ended the sabotage
movement of the early 1960s

Copyright © 1971: GHLLe May
First published in 1971 by BPC Unit 75
St Giles House 49 Poland St London W1
in the British Commonwealth and
American Heritage Press
551 Fifth Avenue New York NY 10017
in the United States of America
Library of Congress Catalogue
Card Number: 71-134599
Made and printed in Great Britain by
Purnell & Sons Ltd Paulton Somerset

BLACK AND WHITE IN SOUTH AFRICA
The Politics of Survival

GHLLe May

To Helen Suzman

American Heritage Press
General Editor: John Roberts

Chapter 1

Slaves and Frontiers

The republic of South Africa originated as a kitchen garden. The metaphor is Lord Bryce's, the reference is to the decision of the Dutch East India Company, in 1652, to occupy the Cape of Good Hope as a refreshment station for their ships. Colonisation was no part of the Company's purpose, yet colonisation followed from the very limitation of its aims. Jan van Riebeeck, the commander of the expedition, was given strict instructions confining him to the provision of water, vegetables, and beef. Some cattle could be bartered from the indigenous inhabitants, a mild race called Hottentots, but van Riebeeck found it cheaper and more certain to provide supplies directly under the Company's control. In 1657 'free burghers' were introduced. Once established, these men began to spread into the interior. They were the original colonists.

The land lay open before them. The Hottentots were swiftly mastered. Two little wars and three epidemics of smallpox destroyed what social cohesion they had as an independent people. They were absorbed as servants or dependants of the white man. Another indigenous people, the Bushmen, were slightly more formidable. They were hunters and food-gatherers, their weapons the bow and the poisoned arrow. They skirmished with the colonists who intruded upon their hunting grounds, but they could make no prolonged resistance. The horse and the gun gave to the Dutch a supremacy in warfare that was not seriously threatened for two centuries. The survivors of the Bushmen drifted away into the deserts. The Hottentots became a landless proletariat. The aboriginals, in short, were swiftly tamed or pushed out. The first 'problem of the non-whites' was of European making. In 1658 the decision was taken to introduce slaves to the Cape. They were brought from East and West Africa, Madagascar, India, Ceylon, and the Malay Archipelago. 'Bushmen, Hottentots, slaves, Europeans — behold the ancestors of the Cape Coloured people.' The first settlers had shown

Left: Cape Town bay at the foot of Table Mountain — a late 18th-century painting. Officially a victualling station for Dutch traders to the East, its outlook became increasingly colonial

A man and woman att the Cape of good Hope

Herberts mount

The Table

E Suger Loaf

K.C

H Jones Antient

Souldanja bay

little prejudice against colour. The line of division was drawn between Christian and heathen rather than between white and black, and the wedding of Pieter van Meerhoff, the Company's surgeon, to a converted Hottentot named Eva had been celebrated as a gala occasion at Cape Town in 1664. It has been suggested that the colour-consciousness of the modern Afrikaner has its origins in the mentality of the slave-owner. The heathen savage had been regarded as a creature of natural inferiority, but savagery was not an irredeemable condition, for the Hottentot might learn the white man's language and habits, and adopt his religion. With slavery, inferiority became structured in a social institution in which status became identified with colour.

The slaves multiplied faster than the settlers. In 1689 the Company sent out between two and three hundred Huguenots—French Protestants who had sought refuge in Holland after the revocation of the Edict of Nantes. This was the sole experiment in systematic colonisation. The Company was a great trading corporation, whose business was profit, not empire. The Huguenots brought to the Cape some new skills, notably the cultivation of the vine. They were quickly assimilated. Their influence can be detected in the prevalence in South Africa of such surnames as de Villiers, du Toit, du Plessis, and Marais. Their children were educated in Dutch, and the French language never established itself.

Whatever the Company might have thought about colonisation, it was forced to recognise the existence of the colonists. Year by year they spread further into the interior. The 18th century saw the evolution of the *trekboer,* the semi-nomadic farmer-rancher, occupying land and moving on when the pasture was exhausted. This was a frontier community unconfined by natural barriers. Not until the neighbourhood of the Gamtoos River, 600 miles to the east, was reached did the colonists impinge upon the Xhosa tribes, the westernmost out-thrust of the Bantu-speaking peoples who today comprise the African population of the republic. There has been much speculation about when the Xhosa arrived, sometimes by scholars seeking facts for their own sake, and sometimes by politicians who felt it important to be able to assert that either the Dutch or the Bantu were the original inhabitants. The evidence is scanty, and comes mostly from the survivors of shipwrecks. It suggests that the Xhosa were established in what is now the Eastern Cape Province in the 17th century. The point is strictly academic—political questions can seldom be settled by reference

Left: Nomadic Hottentot tribesmen resented the Dutch occupation of their pasture-lands. Two wars swiftly subdued them

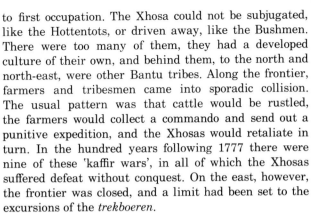

to first occupation. The Xhosa could not be subjugated, like the Hottentots, or driven away, like the Bushmen. There were too many of them, they had a developed culture of their own, and behind them, to the north and north-east, were other Bantu tribes. Along the frontier, farmers and tribesmen came into sporadic collision. The usual pattern was that cattle would be rustled, the farmers would collect a commando and send out a punitive expedition, and the Xhosas would retaliate in turn. In the hundred years following 1777 there were nine of these 'kaffir wars', in all of which the Xhosas suffered defeat without conquest. On the east, however, the frontier was closed, and a limit had been set to the excursions of the *trekboeren*.

The tribal life of the Boer

These inland farmers, by the end of the 18th century, formed almost a sub-culture of their own. They lived close to the soil, in poverty-blighted isolation. They had little learning; the Bible was often their only literature, and they could find in the Old Testament analogues of their own existence. They were Calvinists, but as they lost touch with the settled areas of the western Cape their religion, like their material condition, became crude and simple. The Dutch East India Company was in decline in the 18th century. The longer it governed at the Cape, the laxer its administration became. The Boers of the interior were often left to become a law unto themselves, dealing out rough justice to their slaves and retainers, and sometimes to their neighbours. They expected little from government, except to be left alone. Their grievances were practical and economic—taxes were too high, or the price of cattle too low—and were not expressed in political demands. Their temper of mind was not that of a peasantry but of a primitive aristocracy. It had been noted in the early days of the settlement that the 'free burghers' soon lost the habit of manual labour; one of the results of slavery was that certain kinds of work came to be regarded as unfit for white men. The tradition grew that landholding was the only proper occupation.

It was the strategic importance of the Cape's situation on the sea route between Europe and the Indies that had led to its occupation by the Dutch. The same reason brought the British, who took the Cape by armed force in 1795; they handed it back under the Treaty of Amiens; they came again in 1806, and this time their occupation was to be permanent. The peace settlement which ended the Napoleonic Wars left the Cape as a British colony. The

Left: The pioneers—farmers return from a day's sport, 1801 (top); a settlers' camp on the Great Fish River, 1820 (bottom)

9

British, like the Dutch, had been thinking in maritime terms; they wanted the harbours of the Cape peninsula, and they were not interested in the hinterland. In 1852 the Colonial Secretary reminded the Governor at Cape Town that 'beyond the very limited extent of territory required for the security of the Cape of Good Hope as a naval station, the British Crown and nation have no interest whatever in maintaining a territorial dominion in Southern Africa'. In 1875, when the frontier of European settlement could be drawn a thousand miles to the north of Cape Town, an official in the Colonial Office reported that it had been assumed that the energies of British subjects in those parts would be confined to 'cultivating to their highest capacity the terraced shores of the Southern Ocean'.

The new colony was seldom popular in England. Rider Haggard summed up the prevailing sentiment of nearly a century when he wrote, in 1882: 'The position of South Africa with reference to the mother country is somewhat different from that of her sister colonies, in that she is regarded not so much with apathy tinged with dislike, as with downright disgust.' The Cape produced too little and cost too much. Along with Simon's Bay, Britain had acquired a colonial Dutch population which was by then in jarring contact with the Bantu tribes and had long come to feel neither affection nor gratitude towards the government in Cape Town. The Boers had already spread far beyond the terraced shores. British influence reached them in the unwelcome guise of tax collector, magistrate, missionary, and, generally, interferer in the relations between settler and tribesman, master and servant.

The British brought to the Cape an administrative rigour that was novel to most of the colonists. They governed in accordance with principles laid down in London, and in particular they brought with them a radically different 'official philosophy' towards the coloured population.

There had developed under the Company an attitude that justice was conditioned by status; the British introduced uniform equality before the law. The Dutch were shocked when complaints of ill-treatment of slaves and Hottentots were investigated by a circuit court in 1812. Many of the investigations were instigated by missionaries, and many of the complaints were dismissed as frivolous. The Dutch felt that they should never have come to court at all. A frontier farmer named Bezuidenhout was shot while resisting arrest after he had neglected a summons to appear before a magistrate. His brother led

The movement of the races into the interior of South Africa

Whites

Bantu

Indians

South Africa in 1854

SOUTH WEST AFRICA ✻

0   100   200 mls
0   100   200   300 kms

Right: Maps showing the distribution of Afrikaner, English, and Zulu strength in mid-19th century South Africa (bottom), and the general movement of the races into the interior (top)

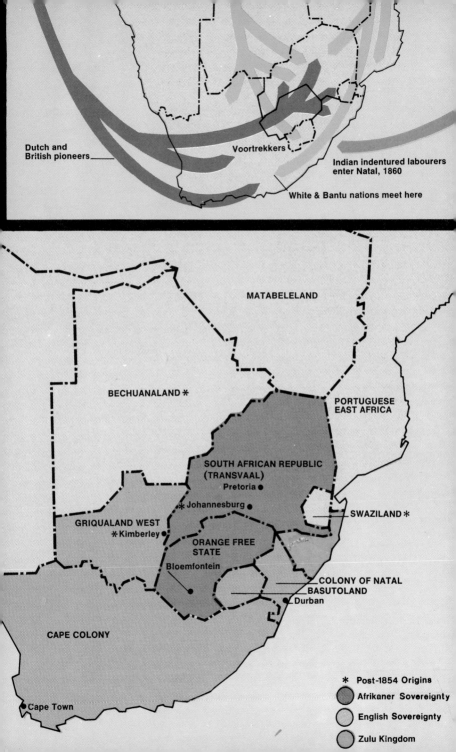

Dutch and
British pioneers

Voortrekkers

Indian indentured labourers
enter Natal, 1860

White & Bantu nations meet here

MATABELELAND

BECHUANALAND *

PORTUGUESE
EAST AFRICA

SOUTH AFRICAN REPUBLIC
(TRANSVAAL)
Pretoria •

* Johannesburg •

GRIQUALAND WEST

* Kimberley •

SWAZILAND *

ORANGE FREE
STATE
Bloemfontein

•

COLONY OF NATAL
BASUTOLAND

• Durban

CAPE COLONY

* Post-1854 Origins

Afrikaner Sovereignty

English Sovereignty

Zulu Kingdom

• Cape Town

a short and unsuccessful rebellion at Slagters Nek, during which he appealed for Xhosa aid.

The Slagters Nek rebellion against the British in 1815 was not a serious threat to the security of the colony, but it provided the Boers with martyrs whose story was later to become a legend: the rope broke at the public execution of the leaders, and the business of hanging was gone through a second time. In 1833 an act of parliament emancipated the slaves — 39,000 of them. The Boers knew little of the changes of opinion in Europe which had condemned this ancient institution, nor had the Cape shared in the development of industry which had made slavery unnecessary as well as inhumane. Not for the last time, the Boers felt that what had changed was not themselves but the world, so that practices once accepted as normal had suddenly become regarded as abhorrent. They simplified the explanation by blaming the missionaries. It was these men, in the Boers' opinion, who had misinformed the British government about the true situation. In this attitude may be found, perhaps, the genesis of the modern Afrikaner's distaste for what he calls 'sickly humanism' and others may call the conventional morality of the world outside South Africa.

The Great Trek

In 1836 there began a mass migration of Boers out of the colony. This was not merely an extension of the nomadic impulse, but a deliberate escape from British rule. Later, this exodus would be known as the Great Trek and the persons who took part in it as the Voortrekkers — the pioneers. The freeing of the slaves was their final grievance, but, as one of them was to write long afterwards, 'it is not so much their freedom that drove us to such lengths, as their being placed on an equal footing with the Christians, contrary to the laws of God and the natural distinction of race and religion . . . wherefore we rather withdrew in order thus to preserve our doctrines in purity'. The government at the Cape let them go, for, as the Attorney-General put it, 'is there any effectual means of arresting persons determined to run away, short of shooting them as they pass the boundary line? I apprehend not. . . .'

But although the British government did not stop the Boers from leaving, it was not prepared to allow them to do as they wished wherever they chose to go. The immedi-

*Far left: Zulu tribesmen from Natal — welded by their leader Shaka into a ruthless fighting nation. **Top left:** A Zulu warrior in full regalia, assegais (long throwing spears) to hand. **Bottom:** Dingaan's brother, rival, and successor Umpanda, who in 1840 became king of the Zulus and accepted Boer rule*

13

ate effect of the Trek was to add a new discord to the problems of the frontier, and to make it more difficult for the British government to maintain its policy of limited commitment in South Africa. The colonist was the burden of empire. If he were left to protect himself against the marauder and the cattle-raider, his methods of defence and reprisal could be represented as aggressive cruelty by those who did not have to face his problems. They might also provoke a kaffir war. If he were to be protected by imperial troops, the costs would be greater and the obligations more indefinite than British governments were prepared to undertake. To garrison the frontiers of the colony was regarded as a deviation from British policy. None the less, in the last resort British subjects could not be abandoned to be massacred, even though some might feel that they were the authors of their own misfortunes. The problem took a different shape when viewed by the men on the spot rather than by officials in London. Professor A.P.Thornton has written: 'In the old British Empire, decked with frontiers everywhere that settlers had wandered away from a sea-coast, both a governor and a colonial secretary would have one simple idea in their heads. Their joint policy was to keep matters quiet on the frontier with what means they had. Hot-headed soldiers or angry settlers might wish, as they did at the Cape, to take over that range of hills, cross that one more river, abscond with the contiguous Alsatia in order to pacify it; but officials who had to count pennies knew that new rivers would be found and new hills sighted, to confound them afresh.'

Zulu power

No directives drafted in Downing Street could prevent the frontier from being pushed back in this way. In 1820 a plantation of English men and women was settled in the area around Grahamstown. They formed a new element of friction with the tribes rather than a buffer against them. Now the Voortrekkers were at large in the interior, moving into lands where there was already immense disturbance among the Bantu-speaking peoples. This was a period in which black men fought with black, and confused movements of population had taken place, consequent upon the emergence of the formidable military power of the Zulus under the rule of Shaka.

'The rise of the Zulu kingdom,' wrote Professor L.M. Thompson, 'had repercussions from the Cape Colonial frontier to Lake Tanganyika. Every community throughout approximately a fifth of the African continent was

Right: *Dignified Zulu women in a native* kraal *or village. The Zulus, wrote Livingstone, were 'shrewd, energetic, and brave'*

14

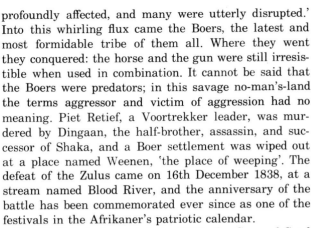

profoundly affected, and many were utterly disrupted.'
Into this whirling flux came the Boers, the latest and
most formidable tribe of them all. Where they went
they conquered: the horse and the gun were still irresis-
tible when used in combination. It cannot be said that
the Boers were predators; in this savage no-man's-land
the terms aggressor and victim of aggression had no
meaning. Piet Retief, a Voortrekker leader, was mur-
dered by Dingaan, the half-brother, assassin, and successor of Shaka, and a Boer settlement was wiped out
at a place named Weenen, 'the place of weeping'. The
defeat of the Zulus came on 16th December 1838, at a
stream named Blood River, and the anniversary of the
battle has been commemorated ever since as one of the
festivals in the Afrikaner's patriotic calendar.

The British had enacted, in 1836, the Cape of Good
Hope Punishment Act, by which they claimed a notional
jurisdiction over the African sub-continent as far up as
latitude 25 degrees south—an area extending 50 miles
north of the modern Pretoria. This claim to supremacy
was in conflict with the policy of limited commitment.
It seemed that the Voortrekkers were drawing the British
behind them in their wake. In 1843 the British annexed
the territory of Natal, with its port of Durban; it was
considered dangerous to permit the Boers to have access
to the sea. Many of the Voortrekkers who had settled
there set out on their travels again. In 1848 an impetuous
British governor annexed the land between the Orange
and Vaal rivers, as the Orange River Sovereignty. Still
there were Boers beyond British rule, established to the
north in what was to be known as the Transvaal. One
British politician described this as 'the strangest race
that ever was run by mortal man' between the escaping
Boers and the pursuing Colonial Office.

The pursuit was, for the moment, nearly over. There
was a swing of opinion in Britain in the 1850s against
the colonies. In 1850 there was yet another kaffir war on
the eastern frontier of the Cape, a serious affair which
dragged on for months and cost the British taxpayer
£3,000,000. The affairs of South Africa were thrust before the British parliament and the outcome was a
return to the policy of limitation. The 'humanitarian
spirit' was in eclipse. There were even some in Britain
who argued that 'the only result of the attempts to
improve these savages has been to give them a taste for

*Left: Calvinism powerfully reinforced the Afrikaner's belief
in his own national destiny. Church Square, Pretoria, is turned into an encampment by local farmers on the occasion
of a special communion service, c. 1870. Pretoria, founded in
1855, was named after Voortrekker leader Andries Pretorius*

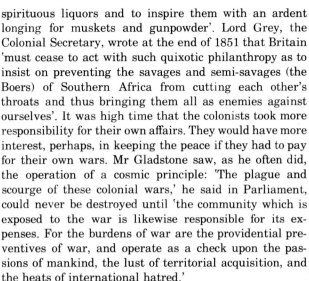

spirituous liquors and to inspire them with an ardent longing for muskets and gunpowder'. Lord Grey, the Colonial Secretary, wrote at the end of 1851 that Britain 'must cease to act with such quixotic philanthropy as to insist on preventing the savages and semi-savages (the Boers) of Southern Africa from cutting each other's throats and thus bringing them all as enemies against ourselves'. It was high time that the colonists took more responsibility for their own affairs. They would have more interest, perhaps, in keeping the peace if they had to pay for their own wars. Mr Gladstone saw, as he often did, the operation of a cosmic principle: 'The plague and scourge of these colonial wars,' he said in Parliament, could never be destroyed until 'the community which is exposed to the war is likewise responsible for its expenses. For the burdens of war are the providential preventives of war, and operate as a check upon the passions of mankind, the lust of territorial acquisition, and the heats of international hatred.'

One result of the new policy was the granting of representative government to the Cape Colony in 1853; the Treasury's desire for economy had more to do with this concession than the operation of any principles of liberty. Another result was the formal recognition of the independence of the Voortrekkers north of the Vaal River. Two commissioners were sent to treat with Commandant Andries Pretorius. One of them, Major Hogge, expressed the mood of the moment: 'The history of the Cape is already written in that of America, and the gradual increase of the white race must eventually though slowly ensure the disappearance of the black. Providence vindicates this its unalterable law by rendering all the philanthropic efforts that have been made to avert such a destiny subservient to its fulfilment.' In effect, the British were saying to the Boers: 'You look after your barbarians and we will look after ours.' By the Sand River Convention of January 1852, Britain conceded autonomy to the 'emigrant farmers' beyond the Vaal. Once Britain had renounced control over the northernmost Boers, there was no logical justification for her continued rule in the Orange River Sovereignty. A new commissioner was sent out in 1854 with instructions to withdraw. There were now two new states in South Africa – the Orange Free State and the Transvaal or South African Republic.

Left: 1879 sounded the death-knell of Zulu independence in a war that cost the lives of 8,000 Zulu warriors and 1,500 Europeans. *Top:* The Natal Native Contingent, officered by Europeans. *Bottom:* The 91st Highlanders return from Zululand, the once-great kingdom now divided into bickering chieftaincies

19

Chapter 2

The Growth of Afrikaner Nationalism

The Great Trek was the most important single event in the history of the Afrikaner people. By the establishment of their republics, it seemed that the Voortrekkers had achieved the aims which they had set before themselves when they left the Cape. They had land in abundance, they had the geographical isolation which they valued and, above all, they were independent of Britain and free to 'preserve their doctrines in purity'. Their success meant that there were now two distinctive philosophies of government in South Africa, each with a different attitude to colour. 'In its most important and most distinctive aspect,' wrote Professor J.S.Marais, 'the Great Trek was nothing else than the rebellion of the Boers against the ideas of the philanthropists. It led to the establishment of two resentful republics where the old Boer attitude to people of colour, an attitude in utter contrast to the post-1828 "Cape tradition", took deeper root.'

The essence of the Cape tradition lay in the equality of all men before the law. The franchise was based upon a property qualification. There was no strong movement to exclude non-whites even after 1872, when the colony achieved responsible government and became effectively independent. The colony of Natal stood midway between the Cape and the republics. The Royal Charter of 1856 proscribed only economic qualifications for the franchise, but only a few non-whites ever found their way on to an electoral register. In Natal, a new racial group had appeared, the Indians. They were brought to South Africa directly to serve the interests of the European sugar-growers, who were finding it difficult to obtain Zulu labour. About 6,000 indentured Indians arrived in 1860, one third of them women. The conditions of their employment made it practically certain that they would become part of the established population: after five years they were free of their indentures and could work where they chose. After ten years they were entitled to a free passage back to India or, if they chose to remain, land to the equivalent value of the passage.

Left: The ox-waggon symbolised the spirit of the Great Trek

21

Most chose to remain, and their numbers were increased by 'passenger' Indians – those who had come to South Africa without indentures, usually as traders. The Indians quickly became integrated into the economy of Natal. They worked as domestic servants, tailors, laundrymen, and artisans; many cultivated fruit and vegetables; others showed high talent as traders. The Europeans who had brought them to South Africa found them both necessary and obnoxious. 'The self-interest of the European brought the Indian to South Africa,' wrote Jan Hofmeyr later; 'self-interest has sought to get rid of him from the country; self-interest, in so far as this cannot be achieved, is determined to keep him in what is regarded as his place.' In their attitude to Indians, the Europeans of Natal displayed a racial prejudice which was in contrast to the liberalism of the Cape, but did not go as far as the deliberate, legally-enforced racial discrimination of the Boer Republics.

The Voortrekkers had been self-chosen by a form of natural selection in reverse. They represented that part of the community of the Cape which was least able to come to terms with the new situation posed by the arrival of the British, and the imposition upon the colonial society of such concepts as legal equality. The original constitution of the Transvaal Republic – the northern and more primitive of the two – stated: 'The People desire to permit no equality between people of colour and the white inhabitants, either in Church or State.' The word 'people' (*volk*) was used restrictively, in the sense of 'our own people', or 'we Boers'. The Orange Free State settled down quickly under regular government. At the end of the century, Lord Bryce was to praise this state as a model republic in which racial bitterness between Boers and the colonial English scarcely existed. The Transvaal was a wilder land. It was some time before regular government appeared, even of a rudimentary kind. For nearly twenty years after the Sand River Convention, there was dissension between different Transvaal leaders, which spread to their followers.

It might seem that the country was made up of primitive family groups, each prepared to go its own way when it could not agree easily with its neighbours. All the Transvaalers were Calvinists, but three branches of the Dutch Reformed Church were established among them. This was not so much a political society as a series of loose family alliances. It was as if these men had taken literally the injunctions of Abram: 'And there was a strife between the herdmen of Abram's cattle and the

Right: Cape Town in 1866, centre of the British 'liberal' tradition which proved so hostile to the Boers' way of living

herdmen of Lot's cattle . . . And Abram said unto Lot,
Let there be no strife, I pray thee, between me and
thee, and between my herdmen and thy herdmen; for we
be brethren. Is not the whole land before thee? Separate
thyself, I pray thee, from me: if thou wilt take the left
hand, then I will go to the right; or if thou depart to the
right hand, then I will go to the left.' *(Genesis xiii.)*

The emergence of the Afrikaner nation

This scattered community was an unlikely breeding
ground for any self-conscious nationalism, a sentiment
which tends to appear in opposition to another racial
group of equal or superior status. The awareness of
Afrikanerdom first appeared in the Cape Colony. As so
often in Europe, nationalism first took the form of demands for language rights. English had been the sole
official language of the Cape since the 1820s. Dutch was
still taught in schools in the towns, but it was a dying
language, competing unsuccessfully with English in
the towns and the vernacular spoken in the country
districts, known as the *taal*. The colonial Dutch formed a
majority of the European population; nonetheless they
were a political minority. The legislative assembly was
dominated by men of English origin. This did not matter
very much during the middle years of the 19th century,
when there were few lasting political issues, but the
situation changed in the 1870s, after the discovery of
diamonds at Kimberley and the growth of the first large
South African industry. Four years after the discovery,
the population of Kimberley had grown to 50,000. Here
was a brawling community of adventurers of all kinds.
Whites were lured by the hope of affluence, black men by
the certainty of high wages, spent often enough on fire-
arms and ammunition. The riches of Kimberley flowed
into many hands, including those of a new generation of
gun-runners.

The discovery of diamonds had its place among the
other factors that contributed to the development of a
new spirit of exclusivism among the Cape Dutch. They
felt that there was something in the new industrialism
that threatened their security; the rapid changes that
accompanied the British on their first arrival seemed
to be repeating themselves. The first nationalist organisations were protective in character. The *Genootskap van
Regte Afrikaners* (Fellowship of True Afrikaners) was
formed in 1875, and stood for 'our language, our nation,
and our country'. It set out to promote the concept of

Top left: *Little England—scene at a club in Port Elizabeth,
1867.* **Bottom:** *Cecil Rhodes with members of a Scots regiment,
1875—already dreaming of an empire from Cape Town to Cairo?*

Afrikanerdom, and had a strong anti-British flavour. The moving spirit was Stephanus du Toit, who campaigned for the formal recognition of the Afrikaans language, a scholarly version of the *taal*.

The development of the movement followed lines which will be familiar to students of European nationalism — the publication of a journal, the rewriting of history, the insistence on the use of the vernacular language in the schools, and then the direct entry into politics. The Genootskap published a contentious 'history of our country in the language of our people'; it made great play with such episodes as the almost legendary rebellion of Slagters Nek. The Genootskap worked for the formation of a specifically Afrikaner outlook upon society, taught in Christian National schools, and expressed in the Afrikaners' own language. In 1879, the movement was extended by the formation of the *Afrikaner Bond* (League of Afrikaners). The success of this movement was in part due to a wave of sympathy among the Dutch of the Cape for the fate of the Transvaal, which had once more become a British colony.

The annexation of the Transvaal in 1877, its occupation, and the revolt of the Boers three years later in the war of Majuba (which led, eventually, to the Convention of Pretoria in 1881, and the granting of virtual independence from British rule), were the most important events to contribute to the growth of Afrikaner nationalism. Nationalism was a reaction to British supremacy, to the concept of imperialism. Ironically, the original reason for the renewed advance of the British towards the north had not been a desire for new territory but an attempt to consolidate the two republics and the two colonies of South Africa into a federation. This accomplished, Britain hoped to be able to limit her own commitments again.

The struggle for the Transvaal

The occasion of the annexation of the Transvaal was a disastrous little war fought by the Transvaal Republic against Sekukuni, a rebellious chief of the Pedi tribe. The Boers were at odds with each other before the expedition against Sekukuni set out. After an initial failure, they became mutinously discouraged. The incident was magnified by rumour into a calamitous defeat. It could be argued that the weakness of the Transvaal might provoke that long-feared South African calamity, the concerted rising of the native peoples to 'sweep the white man into the sea' (John Buchan was evoking deeply-rooted sentiments when he wrote *Prester John*).

Left: The defence of Rorke's Drift, 22nd January 1879: eleven Victoria Crosses were won in this episode in the Zulu war

It seemed to the British government that the Transvaal must be saved from itself. It was bankrupt and drifting towards anarchy. Lord Carnarvon, the Colonial Secretary, was hoping to repeat in South Africa the success which he had enjoyed in promoting federation in Canada in 1867. If the Transvaal could be encouraged to invite a British occupation, one of the obstacles to a closer South African union would have been removed. The Boers had previously made it clear that they had no particular objection to confederation, provided that they kept their independence as well. In Carnarvon's mind, the hoped-for sequence of events would be annexation of the Transvaal, a confederation of South Africa, and then a gradual withdrawal of British influence from those South African questions where an imperial interest was not directly affected. One step forward would be followed, in the fullness of time, by two steps back.

In the event, the annexation was a disastrous mistake. It was carried out in April 1877, against the protests of the Transvaal government, by Sir Theophilus Shepstone. There was no immediate resistance, although the force which Shepstone had with him amounted to only twenty-four mounted policemen. British rule lasted for less than four years. At the end of 1880, the Boers of the Transvaal rose in revolt. They defeated a British regiment at Bronkhorstspruit, north of Pretoria, and then inflicted three defeats on Sir George Colley, commanding the relieving force attempting to force its way into the Transvaal from the south.

The final Boer victory at Majuba Hill in February 1881 cost the British forces 92 men dead and 134 wounded. The Boers lost one man killed and five wounded. As a battle, Majuba was insignificant; as a symbol of Boer success, it was very important indeed. To the Boers, this was the *Eerste Vryheidsoorlog,* the First Freedom War (the second was the war of 1899-1902). The Convention of Pretoria of 1881, modified by the Convention of London of 1884, restored the Transvaal Republic. It was, in many ways, a different society from that which Britain had annexed in 1877. It had a new cohesion, developed by the habit of resistance to the British intruder. It had the memory of success in battle. It had also found a leader, Paul Kruger, the most stubborn and resolute of the opponents of British rule.

The experience of the Transvaal had given a stimulus to the developing Afrikaner consciousness of the south.

Far left: Stock exchange dealings in Johannesburg at first took place in the open. Gold on the Witwatersrand gave birth to the city in 1886. **Left:** Morning market in Kimberley. The new-found riches altered the course of South African history

The Orange Free State had remained neutral during the war of 1880-81, but there was no doubt where its sympathies lay, and individual citizens had joined the Transvaalers as volunteers. In the Cape, Afrikaners were united by sympathy with the Transvaal; the Bond gained in strength and began to be a significant force in politics.

The gold rush
The Transvaal had hardly regained its independence when it found itself threatened once more, this time by what amounted to an industrial revolution. In 1886 gold was found on the Witwatersrand, south of Pretoria. Within ten years, the new city of Johannesburg had a population of 100,000 of all races, half of them Europeans — from the other South African territories, from England, France, the United States of America, and Germany. The Witwatersrand gold fields became a cosmopolitan enclave in the midst of a pastoral state. The Transvaal experienced simultaneously a population explosion and the sudden arrival of an advanced form of capitalised industry. The Boers called the newcomers *Uitlanders* — men from outside. President Kruger saw in their presence a more enduring threat to the independence of his republic than the British government had ever posed. There were few doctrines that could be preserved in purity in the neighbourhood of Johannesburg, a city which a Cape politician contemptuously described as 'Monte Carlo superimposed on Sodom and Gomorrah'.

The Uitlanders developed grievances, some of them real, others of them exaggerated or imagined. Only 40 miles separated Johannesburg from the capital city of Pretoria, but to move from one to the other was to enter a different world. A traveller in time would have noted little in the Boer way of life in the 1880s that was essentially different from that practised a century earlier. Now the Transvaalers were confronted with a new population, almost as numerous as themselves and differing from them in language, beliefs, and purposes. The Boers took practically no part in the new industry. They might sell their land to the great mining combines, and some of them were touched by the streams of affluence which flowed from the gold fields. In the main, however, they regarded Johannesburg as a city of the plain. An Athenian would have understood the connotation of the word 'Uitlander'; it meant 'barbarian'. At the same time, this was precisely how the Uitlander regarded the Boer.

Kruger saw one side of the case with devastating clarity: the survival of the Boers was at stake. He was not prepared to see his own people swamped by alien voters.

Right: Prospectors with African workers sift for diamonds

Independence could be lost perhaps more surely through the ballot box than by the intrusion of a troop of horse. The electoral laws of the Transvaal were altered, so that Uitlanders should not receive full political rights until they had been in the country for fourteen years, and then only after an elaborate procedure of registration.

The Jameson Raid

At the end of 1895 a party among the Uitlanders turned to armed conspiracy. A rising in Johannesburg was to be supported by a force from outside—police from the British South Africa Company's territory to the north.

In 1889 the British government had granted a charter to the Company—headed by Cecil John Rhodes—giving almost unlimited rights and powers of government in the huge area north of the Transvaal and west of Mozambique. In 1890 Rhodes became Prime Minister of the Cape Colony, and was supported in his policy of South Africa for the South Africans by both British and Dutch elements, including the Afrikaner Bond. Leander Jameson, a close friend of Rhodes, was made administrator of the South Africa Company's territories in 1891. Rhodes had hoped that the Boer republic would soon be obliged to enter into closer economic and political relations with the areas under his own control. However, when his repeated efforts at negotiating a customs union with President Kruger met with no success, Rhodes turned his attention to supporting the rebellious Uitlanders in Johannesburg. He financed a revolutionary movement against Kruger's government, but the episode, which came to be known as the Jameson Raid, turned out a tragic farce. There was little secrecy among the conspirators. Anyone who visited the Rand Club in Johannesburg could have discovered that a plot was being hatched. Kruger's attitude was characteristic. He was often asked, he said, about the threatened rising. 'Wait until the time comes; for, take a tortoise, if you want to kill it, you must wait until it puts out its head.'

In December, the tortoise obligingly did so. The Johannesburg rising never took place. Nonetheless, Jameson 'upset the apple cart' (as Rhodes put it) by invading the Transvaal with a private army of no more than 660 men. The raiders were rounded up and captured by a Boer commando on the outskirts of Johannesburg. Jameson himself was handed over to the British government, and the leaders of the Johannesburg conspiracy were **37** ▷

Right: The jagged outline of a Kimberley mine in 1872, staked out with claims. *Next page:* At the battle of Isandhlwana (1879) the Zulus inflicted on the British the worst defeat a modern army has suffered at the hands of men without guns

32

tried in Pretoria. Four of them, including Rhodes's brother, were condemned to death, but, like others who were sentenced to imprisonment, were allowed to ransom themselves. Kruger made no martyrs; indeed, he could appear both as a martyr himself and as the champion of Afrikanerdom. Naboth had successfully defended his vineyard; David had once more vanquished Goliath.

The effects of Jameson's escapade were calamitous for relations between the Transvaal and the British governments, and between Afrikaners and the colonial English throughout South Africa. There was a violent division of political allegiances—for Kruger or against him. Old quarrels were revived. One Boer notable is said to have brought to the Transvaal what was reputed to be the gallows beam of Slagters Nek, so that the Johannesburg conspirators might be hanged from it in retribution. Four years later, the accumulated grievances of Afrikaners against the British were published in a book entitled *A Century of Wrong*. The author was a young Afrikaner from the Cape, Jan Christiaan Smuts, who, after an academic career of astonishing brilliance at Cambridge, had entered colonial politics as a supporter of Rhodes. The main task in South Africa, Smuts then thought, was to unite Englishman and Afrikaner. The Raid was too much for him; he left for the Transvaal and offered his formidable talents to President Kruger. Thousands of his fellow Afrikaners who stayed at home felt as Smuts did in their hearts. Kruger's republic had become a focus of emotion for many who were legally British subjects. On the other side, the growing spirit of Afrikaner nationalism was matched by a hardening of 'jingoism' among the colonial English, who threw their sympathies behind the Uitlanders and regarded Rhodes and Jameson as national heroes. Roger Casement, a young consular official, reported thus on the temper in Johannesburg in the year after the Raid: 'At present most Englishmen in the Transvaal strike me as being loyal [to Britain]; but there is certainly a widespread feeling of regret at what they call the "climb-down" since the beginning of the year. They don't reason—they only feel—and their feeling was expressed by one the other day whose summing up of the situation was that England had allowed a miserable little country like the Transvaal to put its fists in her face: "and if a man did it to me—by Jingo!" '

The Boer War came in 1899. The final question on which negotiations between the British government and the Transvaal broke down was the Uitlander franchise. At a

Left: The Boer war—burghers during a lull in hostilities. To Afrikaners this was the second vital war of independence

deeper level, the Boers fought because they believed that there was no middle way between war and the loss of their independence, the British because they believed that their supremacy in South Africa could be maintained only if they destroyed Afrikaner nationalism at its source. Technically, the Boers were the aggressors, in that they sent the ultimatum. Had they waited a little longer, however, they would have received a British ultimatum. In 1896 Joseph Chamberlain, the Colonial Secretary, had justified a pacific policy towards the Transvaal with the words: 'A war in South Africa would be one of the most serious wars that could possibly be waged. It would be in the nature of civil war. It would leave behind the embers of a strife which, I believe, generations would hardly be long enough to extinguish.' Three years later, Chamberlain had come to agree with his High Commissioner in South Africa, Sir Alfred Milner, that the risk was worth taking.

Sir Alfred Milner, one of the last of the great proconsuls of the British Empire, had enjoyed a brilliant career at Balliol College, Oxford. Thereafter, he had served in Egypt under Lord Cromer, and in the Inland Revenue Office in London. He was sent to South Africa as High Commissioner and Governor of the Cape Colony in 1897, when he was forty-three. His imperialism consisted essentially in the belief that, if Britain were to remain a great power, it was necessary to maintain the integrity of the Empire. This, he believed, was threatened in South Africa by the existence of the South African Republic. There was no room in South Africa for rival nationalisms: he was determined to 'break the dominion of Afrikanerdom' and then to transform the Transvaal by planned settlement, into a British colony.

Those hopes were to be grotesquely disappointed. The course of the war, and its aftermath, justified all Chamberlain's original fears. The sympathies of Britain's Afrikaner subjects were overwhelmingly with the Transvaal and its ally, the Orange Free State. There were two rebellions in the Cape Colony. A future Prime Minister of the Cape, John Merriman, prophesied in 1900 that 'England is going to lose South Africa, and something much worse is going to happen—South Africa is going to lose England. England can afford to lose South Africa, but South Africa cannot afford to lose England.'

The war dragged on for thirty-one months. In all, the British put over 450,000 men into the field in the largest overseas campaign that they had ever conducted. The

Top left: Boers manning the trenches during the siege of Mafeking. *Bottom left:* Boer Amazons helped defend Newcastle, Natal. *Left:* A Boer commando temporarily occupies the town

Orange Free State and the Transvaal were formally annexed in 1900. President Kruger fled to Europe, but the Boers continued the struggle until May 1902. The last stages were extremely bitter. The British commanders-in-chief, Lord Roberts and after him Lord Kitchener, burnt the farms of Boers serving with the commandos. Lord Kitchener carried the process further, by 'clearing the country', much as General Sheridan had done in the Shenandoah Valley during the American Civil War. Boer refugees were confined in concentration camps and over 20,000 of them died there of disease. The peace that was eventually negotiated at Vereeniging in 1902 was made on terms very different from the 'unconditional surrender' which the British had demanded in 1900. The Boers obtained two concessions which they regarded as essential for their survival. One was security for the Dutch language, the other was an assurance that the question of giving the vote to 'natives' would not be decided until after the introduction of self-government. This made it certain that the liberal tradition of the Cape would not be imported into the two new colonies.

The years following the war marked the Afrikaners' darkest hour. They were defeated, and divided among each other between 'bitter-enders' and 'hands-uppers' – those who had fought to the last, and those who had surrendered easily and collaborated with the British. The final debates at Vereeniging had shown, too, angry differences between the Boers of the Orange Free State, who considered that the war should go on, and those of the Transvaal, who had insisted on making peace while there was still time to bargain. At those debates, General Smuts (who had shown a marked and unsuspected capacity for military leadership) made what was perhaps the most persuasive speech of his life. For the sake of their future survival, he said, the Afrikaner nation must accept the defeat that was staring them in the face. If they continued the struggle, they would bring upon themselves their utter destruction. 'It is,' he said, 'as a nation, and not as an army that we are met here, and it is therefore for the nation principally that we must consult . . . From the prisons, the camps, the grave, the *veld*, and from the womb of the future, that nation cries out to us to make a wise decision now . . . We must not sacri-

Top left: *French views of British double-talk – Lord Kitchener proclaims the success of the pacification programme, 'avoiding bloodshed'* **(left)** *and an English soldier displays his 'proverbial gallantry' at a concentration camp* **(right)**. *The hardships of the camps, which were improvised to cordon off Boer refugees from the worst ravages of war, left a deep scar on the Afrikaner mind.* **Bottom:** *British forces cross a river*

41

fice the nation itself on the altar of independence.'

The Boer War had not destroyed Afrikaner nationalism, it had hardened it. 'Afrikanerdom was not broken in the field. It had been strained to the limits of cohesion; but the fibres had held together. In the event, the memory of the war, carefully nurtured as it was, did more to unite Afrikanerdom than Kruger had ever succeeded in doing. The war gave Afrikaners throughout South Africa common victims to mourn, common injuries upon which to brood, a common cause in the restoration of republicanism, and, in the tragic figure of Kruger, dead in exile, a martyr around whom myths could be woven.' The struggle was continued by peaceful means, against Milner's policy of anglicisation. Afrikaners set up their own 'Christian National' schools, rather than place their children under English teachers. 'Milner,' wrote Smuts, 'has dreamed a dream of a British South Africa, loyal in broken English, and happy with a broken heart.' Nonetheless, Milner had failed almost as soon as he had begun. He had hoped for a massive immigration of Englishmen into the former republics, an influx which never occurred. He was faced on the one hand by the sullen resistance of the Afrikaners and on the other by the hostility of the colonial English, the former Uitlanders, who clamoured for political rights and self-government. Self-government was one of the promises which the British had made at Vereeniging, and it could not be delayed indefinitely. Ironically, the pre-war position of Boers and Uitlanders had been reversed. Then, political rights for the Uitlanders would have given them power, now, self-government would mean power for the Boers.

The risk was taken by the Campbell-Bannerman Liberal government after the British general election of 1906. The new colonies could not be governed indefinitely by force. Magnanimity, as Burke had written, might be the truest policy. In 1907, the Transvaal went to the polls; the result was a clear victory for *Het Volk*, the Boer party. In the old Orange Free State, likewise, *Het Volk's* counterpart, the *Oranje Unie,* had an outright majority. In the Cape, John Merriman had formed a coalition ministry which included four members of the Afrikaner Bond in a cabinet of seven. Only in Natal was the 'imperialist party' still in office.

The first stirrings of the colour problem

It might seem that, in the Transvaal at least, the policy of magnanimity had succeeded. General Louis Botha, leader and founder of *Het Volk* and prime minister, was almost fulsome in his gratitude. His policy was one of conciliation between English and Afrikaner. But magnanimity was for whites only; the franchise was not ex-

tended to any persons of colour. The word 'native' in the terms of the peace settlement was extended to include Coloureds and Indians. The African Political Organization, formed in the Cape by Coloured men after the war, to press for the extension of the Cape franchise throughout South Africa, sent a delegation to London to argue their case, without result. The British government had become convinced that, whatever its own opinions might be, the South Africans must be allowed to work out the problem of colour for themselves. In time, perhaps, prejudices might soften, and South Africa take its example from the Cape rather than the Transvaal.

But how firmly based was 'Cape liberalism'? There were already many influential men in that colony who were beginning to draw a distinction between the Coloureds, a minority, and the Africans, an overwhelming majority. In 1895, the *Cape Times*, the mouthpiece of the 'British party', published an article in which may be seen the dim outlines of what, half a century later, would be called the theory of apartheid. Edmund Garrett, the author, wrote: 'Ought we to put resolutely before us the ideal of equality and try to act up to it, or should we . . . frankly recognise that between us and our coloured countrymen (the very word sounds odd to a South African ear) a great gulf is fixed, and never try to overpass it? . . . The one clue to the maze, we think, is to substitute as far as possible the conception of difference in kind for that of difference in degree. Say not that we are superior and they inferior . . . but simply that we are *different,* and that the difference involves, as a matter of practical comfort and convenience for both colours, a certain amount of keeping to ourselves. Of course, we shall go on thinking ourselves the superior race; but it is quite open to our coloured friends to do the same . . . And we are convinced that to err in the opposite direction—to force the trial of these delicate issues on every pretext and to press a pretended amalgamation in social forms where no real one exists—is to challenge that American bitterness of feeling to which South Africa is happily a stranger.'

Left: *The men who reflected the historical divisions of South Africa.* **Left-hand column from top:** *President Kruger of the Transvaal, President Steyn of the Orange Free State, General Botha—the conciliator who became first Prime Minister of South Africa, General Hertzog, who broke with Botha to form the Afrikaner Nationalist Party.* **Right-hand column:** *Lord Milner, Leander Jameson, Generals de Wet and Beyers—Boer war heroes who refused in 1914 to fight 'England's wars'*

Chapter 3
The Status
of the Afrikaner

Eight years after the end of the Boer War, the four colonies—the Cape Colony, Natal, Orange River Colony, and Transvaal—came together in the Union of South Africa. Earnest men and women had been talking about 'closer union' for the past fifty years, but local rivalries and jealousies had kept the communities apart. As long as the two republics remained in being, there was little chance that the descendants of the Voortrekkers would choose to re-enter a British Empire from which they had been at such pains to escape. A shrewd politician might have calculated, by 1910, that the future of South Africa lay with the Afrikaner—provided that he was not swamped by the Bantu or divided against himself. General Smuts saw, no less clearly than Milner had done, that the future of South Africa would be determined in the Transvaal. It was for this reason that he preferred a unitary state to a federation.

The Act of Union was passed by the British parliament, but its terms were entirely drawn up in South Africa, by a national convention of delegates from the four colonies. The Cape tried to extend its franchise to the country as a whole, but there was no support from the other provinces, and the Transvaalers made it clear that they would prefer to break up the convention rather than agree to any extension of the political rights of the non-whites. The Cape kept its own mixed franchise; elsewhere the vote was confined to white men over the age of twenty-one. It was agreed that voting rights might not be diminished without the vote of two-thirds of the members of both Houses of Parliament, meeting in joint session. This was one of the 'entrenched clauses' in an otherwise flexible or uncontrolled constitution. Another laid down that English and Dutch (later, Afrikaans) would have equal status as official languages. Membership of parliament was reserved for whites. In 1910, General Botha became the first Prime Minister. The South African Party (founded that year by Botha and James Hertzog)

Left: General Joubert and staff: the Peace of Vereeniging did not appease the hardline Afrikaner but made him more wary

which supported him contained, at first, nearly all the Afrikaners and a fair proportion of the 'moderate English'. At the first general election it polled 52 per cent of the votes and gained 68 seats in a house of 121. The Unionist Party (founded by Jameson, that May), English and 'imperially-conscious', formed the official opposition, polling 30 per cent of the votes and gaining 37 seats. The remaining seats were scattered amongst the independents.

The split within Afrikanerdom

Beneath the surface, however, Afrikaners were deeply divided. Botha and Smuts were now determined that the Boer War was a thing of the past. The republics were dead and had best be forgotten. Their aim was to develop a broad South African nationalism, based on the equal partnership of the two white groups. This was the meaning of Botha's policy of 'conciliation'. Put another way, it could be said that the Afrikaner should be merged in the South African: his survival would be assured not by exclusivism but by absorption in a wider society. This was by no means the opinion of all Afrikaners. There were many who were obsessed with the past, and who could not forget the deaths in battle and in the concentration camps. To men of this temper, Botha and Smuts had become far too anglicised, too careless of the traditions of the *volk*. It was remembered that Botha had spoken well of Dr Jameson, had unveiled a memorial to Cecil Rhodes, had worn knee-breeches at Buckingham Palace, accepted an honorary major-generalship in the British army, and had presented the Cullinan diamond as a coronation gift to George V (he received in exchange a handsome bill from the British Treasury for the diamond's cutting and setting). Some of the fiercer spirits had regarded the peace of Vereeniging as merely a truce; the struggle might be resumed if Britain were involved in a European war.

There had been no union of hearts in 1910. To these men, nationalism meant Afrikanerdom. They found a spokesmen in General James Barry Munnik Hertzog, a former judge of the old Orange Free State who, like General Smuts, had been a successful military leader during the war. He was now in Botha's cabinet, and disposed to challenge the Prime Minister's policy of conciliation. The break between the two men came on the issue of 'South Africa first', the question whether South Africa's interests were to be regarded as paramount, even in the event of a clash with those of the British Empire. Hertzog was forced out of the cabinet. In 1914, he formed a party of his own, Afrikaner, nation-

Right: Johannesburg 1900—the horse still rules the road

46

alist, and exclusive. Significantly, it took the name the National Party. Afrikanerdom was divided. This was the reopening of a debate which has not yet ceased in South Africa, and which is still the central point about which white politics tend to revolve, a debate between Afrikaners about the place which the Englishman shall occupy in the country.

Hertzog was a complex man, autocratic in temper, subtle of mind, logical, and with a disposition to seek for final solutions to political questions. His dominating motive was the survival of Afrikanerdom, and his speculations upon this aim took him far into the future. In the long run, the danger would come from the Africans, but that day was not yet arrived and in the meantime there was a peril closer at hand in the presence of the Englishman, the English language, and 'English culture'. As he looked about him, it became all too evident that the Afrikaner was in a position of inferiority in all fields except the political. Englishmen dominated industry, commerce, and the professions. They tended to regard South Africa, the Afrikaner's sole homeland, as if it were an integral part of England. They were men of divided loyalties, who spoke of England as 'home', refused to learn the Afrikaner's language and treated him and his traditions with contemptuous indifference. Moreover, the Englishman shared in a world-wide culture, which was foreign to the Afrikaner.

There was, Hertzog felt, a clear and present danger that the Afrikaner would gradually lose his national identity. He must preserve himself by cultural isolation. This was the background to Hertzog's policy of the 'two streams'. Let the Englishman have his culture, but let him keep it to himself. The Afrikaner must preserve his language, his religion, and the peculiar traditions of his own people. Unity might come in the end, but only when the Afrikaner had achieved equality of status, and when the Englishman had come to show a genuine respect for all that the Afrikaner held dear.

Whatever Hertzog might think of Botha and Smuts, it could not be denied that they were genuine heroes of the war, whose deeds formed part of the heroic past of Afrikanerdom. To the new Nationalists, this feeling of respect was expunged by the conduct of Botha and Smuts in 1914. The outbreak of the First World War was followed, in South Africa, by a serious armed rebellion, led by General Beyers, the commander-in-chief of the Union Defence Force, and involving such legendary figures as General de Wet and General de la Rey. Touched off by

Left: *Pretoria in c. 1928, seat of the Union government. As Kruger's capital it had once distrusted the activities on the Rand*

49

Botha's decision to invade German South-West Africa, the rebellion was an expression of Boer sympathy with Germany, and a reflection of the habitual anti-British feeling in the Afrikaner community. Botha suppressed the rebellion with as little force as he could, using Afrikaner troops wherever possible. The sentences on the rebels were lenient enough, with one exception. Commandant Jopie Fourie, a professional soldier, was condemned to death and executed. Smuts, as Minister of Defence, refused to reprieve him.

Here, indeed, was the *broedertwis*, the quarrel of brothers. The new nationalism had its martyr. Botha and Smuts, who had fired on their own people, had become enemies of the *volk*, who had cast themselves out from the bosom of Afrikanerdom. In the general election of 1915, Hertzog's National Party polled a third of the votes and won 27 seats. The South African Party, with 54 seats in a House which now numbered 130, could govern only because, on the issue of the war, it was supported by the Unionists, who held 39 seats (the remaining seats being divided between the Labour Party and the independents).

Gandhi and the rights of Indians

What part in all this had been played by the non-whites? Very little indeed. Such political activity as there had been was conducted by the Indian minority, which had found a leader of genius in Mohandas Karamchand Gandhi, a young barrister who had come to South Africa in 1893 to act for two Indians who were involved in litigation in the Transvaal, and who was to remain in South Africa for twenty years. Sir Keith Hancock, Smuts's biographer, has described Gandhi's experiences on his first arrival: 'On the day of his disembarkation at Durban he visited a magistrate's court and was ordered to take off his turban. Rather than submit to this affront he left the court and saw himself next day advertised in the newspapers as "an unwelcome visitor". On his journey from Durban to Pretoria (in those days it was by rail and road) he was pushed about by the ticket-collector on the train; and pushed about again by the driver of the coach. In Pretoria he was pushed from the pavement into the gutter. His white tormentors, if only they had known it, were pushing him into politics, with consequences incalculable for the history of South Africa, of India and the world.' In 1894 Gandhi founded the Natal Indian Congress to defend the rights of Indians who were about to be excluded from the franchise on grounds of race. In 1906 he led a movement of protest in the Transvaal, where a movement to restrict the rights of Indians—by extending to them a variation of the 'pass laws' which already applied to Africans—was being

planned. It was there that Gandhi developed the technique which he called 'Satyagraha' — non-violent resistance. He won certain concessions; they were small, but the surprising thing was that they had been achieved at all. He carried on his passive resistance after the Act of Union, leading a strike of Indian coal-miners in Natal and marching them into the Transvaal, where they were illegal immigrants. Again, he won certain concessions. In 1914 he returned to India. 'The saint has left our shores,' Smuts wrote, 'I sincerely hope for ever.'

The 'native question'

In 1912 the Africans formed the first organisation of their own, the South African Native National Congress. A deferential organisation, it adopted the name 'native' instead of 'African' so as not to offend white opinion. It attempted, without success, to gain white sympathy in opposition to the passage of the Native Land Act of 1913, which introduced the principle of segregation in the ownership of land. It was clear from the debates that a consensus had developed among white parties on the 'native question': no equality, and as much segregation as was consistent with the demand for black labour. Smuts justified segregation in a speech in London in 1917. 'We have realised,' he said, 'that political ideas which apply to our white civilisation largely do not apply to the administration of native affairs . . . and so a practice has grown up in South Africa of creating parallel institutions . . . Instead of mixing up black and white in the old haphazard way, which instead of lifting up the black degraded the white, we are now trying to lay down a policy of keeping them apart as much as possible in our institutions . . .' Indeed, one of the essential characteristics of South Africa was the manner in which the different population groups lived, as it were, in different camps, some of them from choice and some from necessity. South Africa, it might have been said, was a geographical expression, a state without a nation, a country inhabited by several races and more tribes, in which a homogeneous multi-racial society had not developed.

If the country were to be governed at all, however, these divisions necessitated a certain degree of compromise in white politics. Once the Afrikaners had been split into the followers of Botha and the followers of Hertzog, it became increasingly difficult for any single party to win a working majority in the House of Assembly. For the first forty years after union, coalition was the necessary condition of government. The original South African Party was a coalition in itself. After the secession of the

Left: General Smuts with a Boer burgher during the 1922 strike

51

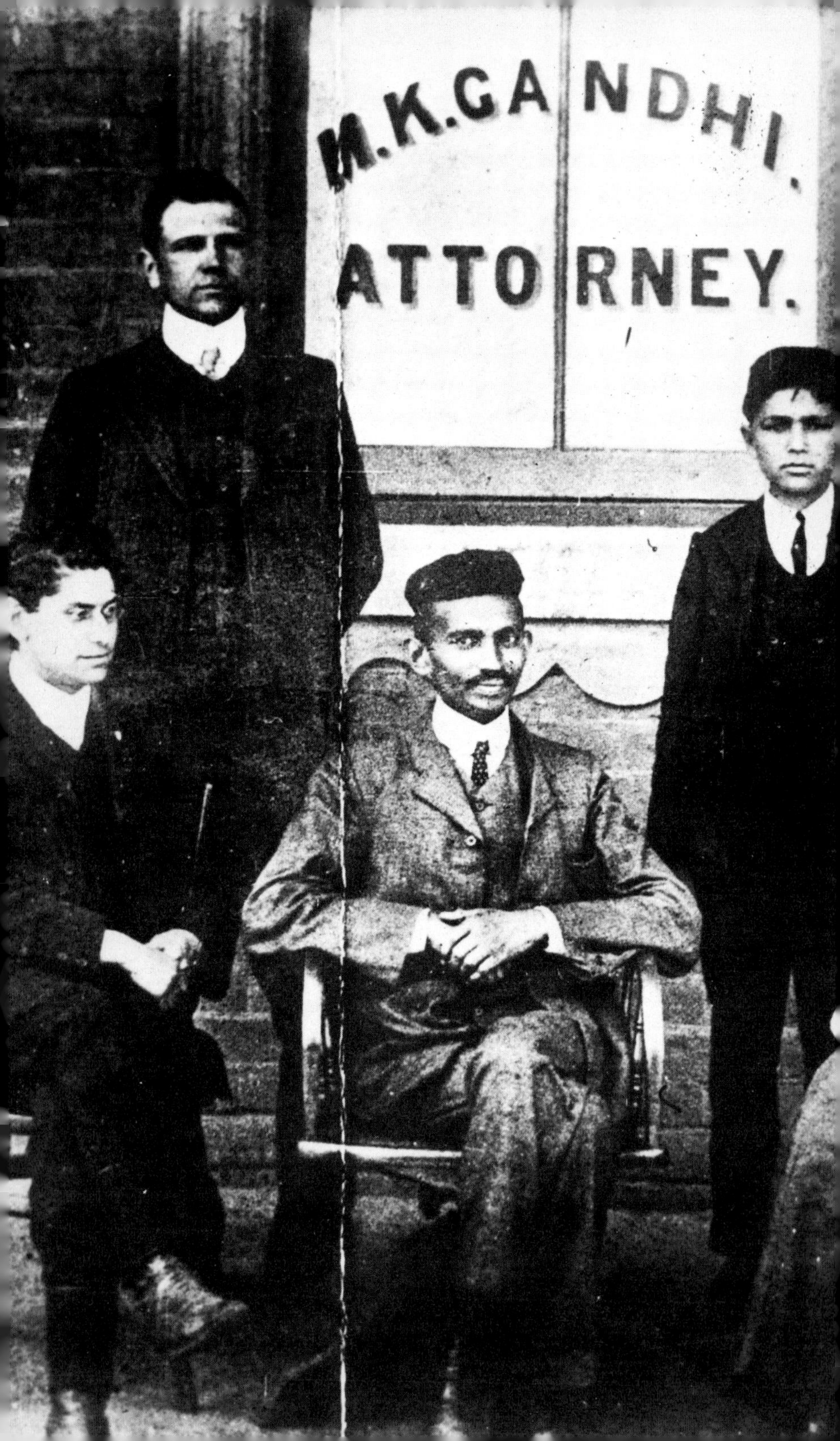
M.K.GANDHI.
ATTORNEY.

Nationalists, the South African Party could govern only because the Unionists were prepared to support it on certain issues. By 1920, the Nationalists had pulled ahead of the South African Party – 37 per cent of the vote against 33 per cent, 44 seats against 41. In that year Smuts came to an arrangement by which the Unionists merged themselves in the South African Party. The enlarged party remained in power until 1924. Then Hertzog became Prime Minister, governing through a pact with the Labour Party (elitist, largely English in membership, highly colour-conscious) which lasted until 1933, when it was replaced with a new coalition, this time between Hertzog and Smuts, whose parties then fused to form the United Party. This split again in 1939, on the issue of South Africa's entry into the Second World War.

Compromise, then, was necessary. For the most part, this was made between white politicians to the detriment of the status of the non-whites. From time to time, appeals were made in parliament and in the press that the 'native question' should be taken out of politics. This usually meant that the opposition of the moment was being invited to agree with the government on how the non-whites should be treated. The non-whites were not a party to the discussion. Indeed, the non-whites were not in politics at all: they were patients, not agents, excluded from the process of making decisions.

It became a standard Nationalist technique to evoke the 'black peril' at election time. *Backveld* audiences of Afrikaners were reassured to be told that their candidate's policy was that of '*die kaffir op sy plek, die koelie uit die land*' (keep the black man in his place, send the Indian back to where he came from). In 1929 General Smuts said in an election speech: 'Let us cultivate feelings of friendship over this African continent, so that one day we may have a British confederation of African states . . . a great African dominion stretching unbroken through Africa.' This was enough for the Nationalists to depict Smuts as the advocate of racial equality, who would submerge South Africa in a sea of colour. Hertzog, Malan, and Tielman Roos (the Nationalist leaders in their respective provinces) produced the *Black Manifesto*, which denounced Smuts as 'the man who puts himself forward as the apostle of a black Kaffir state . . . extending from the Cape to Egypt . . . and already foretells the day when even the name of South Africa will vanish in smoke upon the altar of the Kaffir state he so ardently desires'. This propaganda was effective enough; the National Party won 78 seats to the South African Party's 61 in

Left: Gandhi in South Africa, 1903. His agitation for Asian rights in Natal and the Transvaal helped prepare him for India

the general election of 1929; the South African Party had won more votes – 47 per cent compared with 40 per cent.

The discrepancy between votes cast and seats won is a commonplace occurrence in electoral systems which are based on the single-member constituency and the simple majority vote, especially when, as in South Africa, one party is characteristically urban, the other characteristically rural. But there was an additional cause of distortion built into the South African constitution. In delimiting constituencies, the electoral commissioners were empowered to 'weight' a seat by 15 per cent either under or over the 'electoral quota' (obtained by dividing the electorate of each province by the number of seats to which it was entitled). This meant that there might be as many as 30 per cent more voters in the largest urban than in the smallest rural constituency. This deliberate favouring of the farmer over the town-dweller was consistent with the Afrikaner myth of the corrupting influence of the cities, but it owed its origin to Lord Milner's draft constitution for the colony of the Transvaal in 1904, in which Milner sought to diminish the influence of *Het Volk* by enfranchising the small towns which had substantial British communities.

Early segregation measures
Each successive government made its own contribution to the mass of legislation which imposed a pattern of segregation of whites from blacks. Botha's government had legislated for segregation in the ownership of land. Smuts (who became Prime Minister on Botha's death in 1919) introduced the Native (Urban Areas) Bill of 1923, which provided for residential segregation in towns. The measure did not abandon wholly the traditions of 'Cape liberalism', in that it attempted to draw a line between 'civilised' Africans and those who had not yet 'emerged from barbarism'. Nonetheless, it entrenched in legislation the principle of 'migratory labour', and made clear that Africans were to be encouraged to live in towns only so far as their labour was needed. There was a note of despairing fatalism about Smuts's language: 'The native question is so large. We know so little about it, we know so little about certain factors which seem almost beyond human control.' It was not a question upon which Smuts ever thought very deeply. Towards the end of his life, he saw the problem in terms of prudent paternalism, in which security and material benefits for the Africans would be their compensation for the absence of political rights. His attitude was fully fashioned, when he wrote in 1906 that 'it ought to be the policy of all parties to do justice to the natives and to take all wise and prudent measures for their civilisation and improvement. But I don't believe

in politics for them. . . . When I consider the political future of the natives in South Africa I must say that I look into shadows and darkness, and then I feel inclined to shift the intolerable burden of solving that sphinx problem to the ampler shoulders and stronger brains of the future.'

There were those who hoped that the 'native question' would settle itself in the fullness of time, perhaps by the spontaneous creation of an African middle-class rising upwards on the economic ladder. Against this, there was the strong desire of the white artisans to defend their own position in the labour market against competition from Africans. The Rand Revolt of 1922 was caused in part by the attempt of the Chamber of Mines to replace white labour by black. There was a general strike – with racial overtones – and demands that the government should nationalise the mines. Some of the white strikers carried banners which read: 'Workers of the World, fight and unite for a White South Africa.' The leader of the Labour Party, Colonel Creswell, said that he stood for total segregation as the goal of 'native policy'. The Nationalist-Labour Pact government of 1924 introduced the principle of 'civilised labour' into industry, strengthening the position of the white worker by reserving certain jobs for whites only. At the same time, this government sought to enhance the status of the Afrikaner. There was a long and bitter struggle over the question of the introduction of a distinctive South African flag which, it was eventually decided, would be flown side by side with the Union Jack. Afrikaans superseded Dutch as an official language. Republicanism remained the ultimate goal of the National Party, but this issue was not pressed. Hertzog was satisfied with the imperial developments enacted in the Statute of Westminster in 1931. Sovereignty was then officially granted to the dominions, and with it independence from the jurisdiction of the British government (previously imperial acts had applied, automatically, to all the dominions within the Commonwealth).

The great depression of the 1930s had a disintegrating effect upon the structure of white politics in South Africa. Hertzog's government refused to follow Britain in abandoning the gold standard, partly because of rigid economic principles and partly as a matter of national pride. South Africa would show her independence no less in matters of finance than in those of politics. The result was a grim period of deflation, which produced a challenge to Hertzog's leadership in the person of Tielman Roos, who resigned his position on 'the bench of the

Left: The Earl of Athlone, Governor-General of South Africa, opening parliament, 1926: the British provided the pomp

55

Supreme Court to lead a campaign against the gold standard. Roos succeeded in his immediate aim; South Africa went off gold, and the economy immediately began to recover. Roos had other ambitions. He wanted the premiership, but eventually Hertzog and Smuts composed their differences, and formed the United South African National Party, with Hertzog as leader and Smuts in second position. It might seem that the Boer War was over at last. 'I almost feel,' Smuts wrote, 'as if we are at last through our racial troubles.' The remark was revealing: 'racialism', in the South African vocabulary, referred not to conflicts of colour but to relationships between the English and the Afrikaners.

Smuts's enthusiasm was premature. Seven members of his own following broke away to form the Dominion Party, led by Colonel Charles Stallard. The United Party, they felt, was not sufficiently committed against republicanism. More significant for the future was the secession of part of Hertzog's own following, under Dr Daniel François Malan, a former minister of the Dutch Reformed Church, who had been the first editor of *Die Burger*, a Nationalist newspaper in Cape Town, and then a leading member of Hertzog's cabinet. Malan had overtaken Hertzog on the right, in much the same manner as Hertzog had overtaken Botha. Malan's new party took the name of the Purified National Party, claiming that they, and not the United Party, were the guardians of the *volk*, the true representatives of Afrikanerdom. In the general election of 1938 the United Party won 111 seats in a house of 150, but 30 per cent of the electorate, representing about half of the Afrikaner population, voted for Malan.

Part of the price which Smuts had paid for his reconciliation with Hertzog was an agreement to alter the constitution to remove the African (as distinct from the Coloured) voters of the Cape from the common electoral roll. This was one more attempt 'to take the native question out of politics'. Hertzog had already attempted to do this twice before, in 1926 and 1929. He had been unable then to muster the necessary two-thirds majority of both Houses. The old South African Party had opposed him on the grounds that the agreement of union was a sacred compact. By 1936, however, they had changed their minds. Hertzog introduced his bill as one to prevent the eventual political domination of the black man over the white. He dwelt on the importance of unity among whites

Left: Scenes from the 1922 general strike—troops clear the Johannesburg streets (top left); Africans under escort move their dead from the scene of an attack by Afrikaner strikers (top right); the market square of Fordsburg, a working-class suburb of Johannesburg, after gunnery bombardment (bottom)

57

on this issue: the alternative would be the danger of finding the whites in opposite camps, one section alone and the other having 'millions of natives' behind it. 'Christian principles stood high,' he said, 'but self-preservation stood higher, because it was the only way in which humanity, and Christianity itself, could be defended.'

Hertzog was challenged by his Minister of Education, Jan Hofmeyr, a young man who had established a reputation as an intellectual prodigy (he was a professor at twenty-two, and principal of Witwatersrand University at twenty-four), and who was beginning to be regarded as the foremost exponent of what was left of 'Cape liberalism'. Hofmeyr refused to vote for the bill (though he did not leave the cabinet). The argument that the native should develop along his own lines, said Hofmeyr, was merely another assertion of the old demand that the native should be 'kept in his place'. The educated black man would be driven back upon his own people, but in hostility and disgruntlement, to become a leader in disaffection and revolt. As to the Christian principle of self-preservation, he said, he was reminded 'of the eternal paradox that whosoever will save his life shall lose it'. Hofmeyr was applying to the Africans almost the identical principle that the Campbell-Bannerman government had applied to the Boers, when conceding self-government to the former republics in 1907. It had previously been assumed that the Boer republics should not be granted self-government until they had demonstrated their loyalty to the Empire. Campbell-Bannerman had accepted the argument that colonial dependencies could better be governed by consent than by constraint—that until the Boers were trusted they never would be reconciled.

In the Union of South Africa, Hofmeyr's voice was as one crying in the wilderness. The new act gave the Africans in the Cape three white members of the House of Representatives, and Africans throughout the country the right to elect four members of the Senate. It also created a Native Representative Council, and increased the area of land set aside as 'native reserves'.

What was the reaction of the Africans? They had no political power, and no other effective organisation. The African National Congress (as the 'Native Congress' had renamed itself in 1919) was little more than a debating society. It had summoned an 'All-African Convention', which met in Bloemfontein at the end of 1935, to discuss the bill, and had declared itself dissatisfied. That was as far as effective opposition went.

Left: Two styles of ceremonial greeting for Edward, Prince of Wales, on tour in Zululand in 1925. The chiefs wear uniform

59

Chapter 4
The Genesis of Afrikaner Supremacy

By 1934 it might seem that General Hertzog had won his battle for status. He was satisfied both with the position of the Afrikaner in South Africa and with the position of his country as an independent state. Dr Malan was satisfied with neither. For him, the battle would not be over until the Purified Nationalists ruled over a united republic. Until that day came, he felt, the Afrikaner was still (because of continuing English power in government) a poor relation in what should be the family home. For the moment, the political tide was running against Malan. His party won only 27 seats in the general election of 1938. He could, however, enjoy the luxury of making plans for the future without the distractions and responsibilities of office. It was in the years between 1934 and 1948 that the Nationalists formulated a strategy for the conquest and retention of power. In doing so, they elevated bitterness into an instrument of policy, and transmitted it to a new generation.

The bitterness that followed the Peace of Vereeniging in 1902 had been deep and personal. Those who experienced it had, themselves, suffered very directly. But one after another, the war leaders had come to terms with the British Empire and the South African English. Botha had led the way, followed by Smuts. General Hertzog had, for nearly thirty years, carried on the tradition of President Steyn – the leader of the Orange Free State who, in 1902, would have preferred a Boer suicide-pact to surrender. Now even Hertzog, it seemed, had gone the way of Botha and Smuts. By 1934 a new generation of bitter-enders had arisen, but their bitterness was vicarious, nurtured by many who had not experienced the horrors of the war except in imagination. The veterans had got the war out of their systems, but some of their children could not forget what they had been taught in their formative years. General Hertzog's son could not forgive his father for the

Left: The opening of the Voortrekker Monument near Pretoria by Prime Minister Malan on 16th December 1949, the anniversary of the Battle of Blood River. The monument is as much to the laager mentality as to the memory of the Voortrekkers

reunion with Smuts, and was firmly in Malan's *laager*. Many Afrikaner families were split down the centre. President Steyn's widow had made her peace with Smuts when he decided to serve under Hertzog in 1933 and her son became one of his stalwart followers. Other Steyns went with Malan, and the family met formally only to lay a wreath, once a year, on the old President's grave. To the Purified Nationalist, Smuts was the betrayer of the faith and the Man of Blood, and Hertzog now the Lost Leader. Botha was in his grave, but Smuts could be pilloried in the Afrikaans press as the 'handyman of the British Empire', the lackey of the old enemy.

The birth of the Broederbond

In 1918 a number of 'nationally-minded Afrikaners' formed a secret society which they named the *Broederbond* (League of Brothers). Its aim was said to be the furtherance of the cultural and economic welfare of the Afrikaner, the preservation of his national identity. After Hertzog and Smuts came together in 1934, the Broederbond took on something of the nature of an Afrikaner government in exile. Hertzog's son was a prominent member; so was Professor Hendrik Frensch Verwoerd, who had resigned his chair of sociology in Stellenbosch University to become the first editor of *Die Transvaler,* a National Party newspaper founded in Johannesburg.

The Broeders (to judge from their later success) were men of intellect, imagination, narrow intensity of purpose, and unswerving ambition. They recruited new members with extreme care. In time, they established a network of cells which linked the National Party with the Dutch Reformed churches, the teaching profession, the public service, the army, and the police, and the fields of commerce and industry into which the Afrikaner was beginning to penetrate — in short, with every activity which, in their opinion, might one day come under the domination of Afrikanerdom. In all but doctrine, they had little to learn from the Bolsheviks. They evolved Lenin's techniques of practical organisation for themselves. They mastered the techniques of interlocking control of a host of organisations: the Broederbond was an effective holding company, the progenitor and controller of such organisations as the *Federasie van Afrikaanse Kultuurverenings* (Federation of Afrikaans Cultural Societies), the *Reddingsdaad Bond* (League for the Act of Salvation, a welfare organisation), and many others. They rejected the principles of liberalism — universality, diversity, and tolerance.

Left: *Textile workers on their way to gaol for striking, 1930*

After 1934, the Broederbond, in endless discussion, formulated plans for the future of a South Africa in which the 'right-thinking Afrikaner' should not merely survive but implant his doctrines in the hearts of those who lived in 'his' country. In this context, the National Party was not merely a political organisation but one aspect of a way of life, simultaneously total and exclusive, to be reserved for those who were Afrikaners in blood, language, religion, and outlook. The Broederbond evoked a future both stern and glorious, and dwelt on the memory of a persecuted past: the Lord would not forget those whom he had chastened, nor permit their enemies to rest in peace. General Hertzog denounced the Broederbond with vehemence. Well he might, for it had already numbered him among the backsliders of the *volk* and rejected his policy of 'two streams' and equality between the two white groups in favour of unrestrained Nationalist supremacy.

The Afrikaner had never been afraid of the African as a potential adversary in battle. He showed a serene confidence of superiority in any physical conflict. What he feared was something more insidious — loss of his 'national identity' through contact with the African. Racial mixing was the ultimate peril. One of the reasons which Hertzog had given for the removal of the African voters from the common roll was that the mingling of the races at election time had increased this possibility. This fear gave a particular urgency to the problem of the 'poor whites'.

In the middle of the 1930s it was estimated that about 300,000 Afrikaners — a quarter of their total number — lived on or below the margin of subsistence. This was a problem which the more affluent English section had escaped. 'Poor-whitism' was an old affliction, one of the unhappy consequences of industrialisation. Year by year, unskilled labourers, both black and white, flocked into the growing cities, there to form a proletariat. Segregation broke down in the slums, where the poor of many races might live literally cheek by jowl. It was in the racial hotch-potch of the cities, wrote one sociologist, that the Afrikaner had found his new 'eastern frontier', a new battleground for survival. The poor Afrikaner needed help, but it must come in such a manner that it neither blurred his consciousness of colour nor anglicised him in outlook. In every field, from recreation to welfare, the Broederbond sought to create specifically Afrikaner organisations. It was in the suppressed multitudes of Afrikanerdom that the future lay.

According to Nationalist interpretations of the census figures of 1936, the proportion of Afrikaners to English in

Right: In an atmosphere reminiscent of 1914 Afrikaner workers protest against South Africa's entry into the Second World War

South Africa increased dramatically as one went down the scale of age. Of whites over twenty-one, there were 115 Afrikaners for every 100 English; between seven and twenty-one, there were 185; and under seven, there were 212. The seeds of victory had been sown in the marriage bed. The problem was to secure Afrikaner youth for the National Party. Segregation, economic and social, took on a new urgency. For the South African English, the danger of losing a livelihood to a black competitor was remote. They could view the *swaart gevaar*, the 'black peril' that loomed so large in Nationalist propaganda, with something of the complacency that the middle-classes in Victorian England had shown to the 'other nation' of the poor. For the English, segregation was a question of economics. The Afrikaner 'poor white', on the other hand, needed positive protection: segregation could be regarded as a necessary condition for survival.

The Purified National Party gave an impressive demonstration of the power of its appeal in 1938, the centenary of the victory of Blood River over the Zulus, the year chosen for the celebration of the Great Trek. This was a national occasion only in name; it was transformed into a party festival. At its culmination, on 16th December, the Prime Minister did not attend. Smuts spoke, as a private citizen, and was given a cool reception. It was Malan who emerged as the spokesman and hero of the *volk*. His theme was that the Afrikaner had a new battle of Blood River to win, this time on the field of economic competition.

To fight or not to fight

Malan's political opportunity was provided by Adolf Hitler. Ever since 1914, Nationalists had argued that only the coming of the republic would prevent South Africa from being dragged, willy-nilly, into Britain's wars. Malan was now the keeper of this dogma. To Hertzog, republicanism had receded from the forefront of politics, to become an ideal only to be achieved when it was desired by the great majority of white South Africans, English as well as Afrikaans. Republicanism had no longer any necessary connection with sovereign independence, and it was admitted that South Africa had the right to remain neutral in any future war. The decision would be taken solely in accordance with South African interests. In 1938 the cabinet had agreed that, if war broke out over Czechoslovakia, South Africa should adopt a posture of 'benevolent neutrality' towards Britain, honouring her agreement to allow the Royal Navy the use of the naval base at Simonstown, but not becoming a belligerent herself. In 1939, when Germany invaded Poland, Smuts changed his mind. Hertzog did not. Hertzog's neutrality

motion was defeated by 13 votes in the House of Assembly, but the United Party split down the middle. Forty of its members of parliament, all Afrikaners, voted with Hertzog. Amid scenes of sombre rejoicing, they were welcomed back into the fold of purified Afrikanerdom. A deeply divided country went to war.

The opportunity to reunite Afrikanerdom had come; but this was a fulfilment not to be achieved without struggle and bitter internal dissension. A substantial number of Afrikaners still followed Smuts. The National Party had been swollen by an influx of new recruits of diverse opinions and allegiances. In the *broedertwis* (strife between brothers) of the next few years, Malan appeared as a figure of moderation. Strange groups appeared, such as the *Ossewa Brandwag* (oxwaggon sentinels), a paramilitary organisation which was blamed for acts of sabotage, and whose members brawled from time to time with men in uniform. The recurring debate within Afrikanerdom – the place of the Englishman in a nationalist South Africa – was resumed with an urgent ferocity. A draft constitution for a future republic appeared in 1942, and expressed the views of the Nationalist extremists in the most uncompromising of terms. Hertzog was soon pushed aside. He died, saddened and rejected, in 1942. Smuts's party and its allies won the general election of 1943 comfortably enough. But that election was also a victory for Malan. The Nationalist splinter groups were eliminated and the National Party won 43 seats and a third of the popular vote. Time, they could reasonably feel, was on their side.

One consequence of the war was a general hardening of attitudes, throughout South Africa, on the question of colour. If one theme in South African politics has been the attempt of Nationalist Afrikaners to unite, another has been attempts by non-Nationalists of European origin to come to a compromise, usually at the expense of the non-whites. Part of the price which Smuts paid for his war-time coalition was concession to the English of Natal, who were demanding new restrictions upon the Indian population of that province. It was the imposition of these measures that was to bring South Africa into conflict with the government of India, and to provide the occasion for the first attacks on South Africa's racial policies at the United Nations. The first shocks from without fell upon Smuts. At the same time that white opinion was hardening within South Africa, the non-whites were beginning to formulate demands which could not be met within the existing structure of South African society.

In part, the non-whites were reacting to the industrial

Left: 'Poor whites' in a slum area of Johannesburg, c. 1930

changes which the war had accelerated – inflation, the development of new industries, and a consequent increase in the black labour force. There was a serious wage strike by African mineworkers on the Witwatersrand in 1946. In part, the non-whites in South Africa were influenced by the mystique of the brave new world generated by Allied propaganda, and stimulated by the American hostility to all forms of imperialism which characterised the closing stages of the war. The Atlantic Charter looked forward to the United Nations Declaration of Human Rights, which in turn looked forward to a world purged of fear, oppression, and poverty, in which man's attitudes would be more humane. Anti-colonialism was one of the prevailing moods of the moment, and at the end of the war South Africa suddenly found itself demoted from its war-time status of gallant ally to that of an oppressive power, with a hostile world opinion being mobilised against it. To some American politicians, it seemed that one of the dangers to the future peace of the world lay in 'British imperialism' and that the principles of self-determinism, rejected by the victor powers as applied to their own possessions in 1919, might be applied after the end of the Second World War. To those who held this opinion, it might seem that South Africa was a colonial dependency, which should grant rights to its indigenous inhabitants. Nearly all white South Africans held that they had at least as good a title to possession as any of the African peoples.

Smuts and post-war problems
Smuts was adamant, at the United Nations, in insisting that the internal affairs of South Africa were excluded by the terms of the Charter from international interference. South Africa did not fit into any recognisable colonial pattern. It was a sovereign state made up of former colonies which had achieved independence through amalgamation, with the complication that in doing so it had become a quasi-colonial power in its own right, with subject peoples living within its own boundaries. But neither governors nor governed had anywhere else to go. In this context, it was nonsense to speak of returning a white settler population to its land of origin. There was no metropolitan power abroad which could transfer authority from white to black and the governing whites had no intention of surrendering, or even sharing, power.

Those Afrikaner sociologists who had laid stress on the problem of the cities as the focal point of the politics of survival had diagnosed accurately enough. The census figures told their own story. In 1946, for the first time, the urban African population outstripped the European. In round figures, the urban population consisted of 1,700,000

whites and 1,800,000 Africans, and it was the African population which was increasing more rapidly.

The question is worth asking whether there was a clear alternative before Smuts, in his days of power, which if taken boldly would have placed South Africa upon another course. The answer lies entirely in the domain of white politics. No Prime Minister could have done more than the electorate would permit. It is difficult to see what Smuts could have done, in the time permitted to him. Until the end of the Second World War, the non-white question had never been in the forefront of white politics, where the dominating problem was what was called 'racialism'—the relationship between Englishmen and Afrikaners. Now, a single generation was, as it were, being asked to solve a problem that had been accumulating, in complexity and scale, for generations.

In the short-term there was one thing which Smuts was urged and refused to do—to amend that section of the Act of Union which weighted parliamentary representation in favour of the rural areas. It could be plausibly argued that it had long outlived its usefulness. Smuts had been one of the principal architects of union. He was unwilling to upset any of its provisions, and he seems to have regarded his own position in 1948 as unassailable. Many of his critics had noticed a touch of hubris in his demeanour. Had he amended the clause before 1948, he would almost certainly have won that election. In crude votes he had a substantial majority.

It was one of the Nationalists' charges against the United Party that their 'native policy' was one of drift and neglect. There was much to be said for the Nationalist contention. Smuts himself had little to offer, except high generalisation: the caravan of humanity was once more on the move, and time would take care of all things. What he did not expect was any challenge from inside or outside South Africa to the structure of white supremacy. As a politician, he was never one to move faster than his followers. What he had to offer was, at best, the hope of cautious improvement. He had appointed a commission under Mr Justice Fagan, which reported in 1948, and pointed the way towards a society that should be integrated economically, but segregated socially and politically. In particular, the Fagan Report urged that the urban African should be recognised as a permanent part of the population of the cities, and not treated as a migrant labourer on leave, as it were, from his tribe. The United Party talked in terms of establishing middle-class

Left: African soldiers at Anzio, March 1944. During the war 45,000 Cape Coloured and 80,000 Africans served as drivers and hospital orderlies wherever South African forces operated

69

African townships, in which the man of superior attainment could differentiate himself from the barbarian mass.

Cautious improvement was too little for the African, too much for the Nationalist. Even the docile and conservative Native Representative Council was now talking in terms of rights, and demanding the dismantling of the whole apparatus of racial discrimination. In 1947 Smuts had written, with despairing clarity: 'The fact is that both native and Indian leaders want *status* . . . in social and economic advances we have a strong case, but the natives want *rights* and not improvements. There we bump up against the claim for equality which is most difficult to satisfy except in very small doses which will not satisfy the leaders.' In 1946 the Native Representative Council had passed a resolution deprecating 'the government's post-war continuation of a policy of Fascism which is the antithesis and negation of the letter and the spirit of the Atlantic Charter and the United Nations Charter', and calling upon Smuts 'forthwith to abolish all discriminatory legislation affecting non-Europeans in this country'. This was something which no South African government, with the existing electorate, could do and hope to remain in power.

Victory for the Nationalists

Most general elections are concerned rather with who shall govern than how government shall be conducted, and few are fought upon a single issue. The general election of 1948 in South Africa was no exception. The Nationalists were able to exploit all the accumulated grievances and disenchantments that followed the ending of the war. They dwelt on rising prices and the complaints of ex-servicemen dissatisfied with their civilian status; they attacked Smuts for his preoccupation with world affairs and neglect of his own people. The old cries were repeated about South Africa being dragged into Britain's wars, and play was made of the association with 'godless Communism' at the United Nations ('A vote for Smuts,' declared one slogan, with mysterious logic, 'is a vote for Stalin'). The cartoon figure of 'Hoggenheimer', a bloated capitalist with cigar and diamond rings, made his customary appearance; he evoked the memories of the Jameson Raid, appealed to anti-semitism, and hinted at the subservience of the United Party to the 'money power'. A new enemy appeared — the 'liberalist', portrayed as dupe or

Right: War acted as a spur to industrial expansion; Africans flocked to the cities in search of work and shanty towns like Cato Manor near Durban **(right)** and Newclare near Johannesburg **(bottom right)** created new post-war problems. **Top right:** The Native Army service corps pray in the Western Desert, 1942

ally of Communism, and identified with Jan Hofmeyr, the Deputy Prime Minister: this was a more sophisticated variant of the old rhetorical question, 'How would you like your daughter to marry a native?' There were promises of white bread (brown bread made from wholemeal flour had been introduced as a war measure); there were the customary reminders of the persecution of the Afrikaner in the past and the appeals to the call of the blood. What distinguished the election from others since union was a new promise of survival for the Afrikaner, through 'apartheid'. The electorate might vote from other motives, but it was being offered, almost for the first time, a distinctive choice on the 'native question'.

The United Party based its colour policy on the Fagan Report—the recognition of economic interdependence of the races, coupled with social and political segregation. It was not a spectacular policy. It implied that the development of the economy would produce, in the long run, its own solution which, it was assumed, would not be in conflict with the 'traditional policy' of white supremacy. The Nationalists offered resolute action. 'Apartheid' was a new word in the political vocabulary, but the ideas behind it had been germinating in the minds of Afrikaner intellectuals for the past dozen years. These men had set themselves a problem which might seem analogous to squaring the circle—how could the Afrikaner first, and the white man second, assure his supremacy in a country in which, day by day, he was increasingly in the minority? Their solution involved the adoption of an ideology which would require, if it were to be transformed into reality, a use of the power of the state on a scale never before attempted in South Africa. It would involve not only a mass movement of the population but it would also involve a radical transformation of men's minds and aspirations—not only for the whites, but for the non-whites as well.

The choice before the electorate was presented as a simple alternative—integration (an eventual mixing of races) or apartheid (separation). There was, it was asserted, no middle way: the Nationalists used the argument of the irreconcilable alternative, the logic of the ultimate consequence. 'We can,' said one of their election manifestos, 'act in only one of two directions. Either we must follow the course of equality, which must eventually mean national suicide for the white race, or we must take the course of separation *(apartheid)* through which the character and the future of every race will be protected . . . the [National Party] therefore undertakes to protect the white race properly and effectively against any policy,

Left: *Police and African mineworkers clash during the Witwatersrand wage strike, 1946. World opinion turned sour*

73

doctrine or attack which might undermine or threaten its continued existence. At the same time the party rejects any policy of oppression and exploitation of the non-Europeans by the Europeans as being in conflict with the Christian basis of our national life and irreconcilable with our policy.'

Elaborated in more detail, apartheid promised barriers not only between whites and non-whites but between the different non-white peoples. The Cape Coloureds would be isolated from whites on one hand and Africans on the other. The Indians, the familiar scapegoats, were described as a 'foreign element' which could not be assimilated. It would be best if they went back to India. While they remained, they could not expect treatment other than that appropriate to an unwanted immigrant group. As for the African majority, they would develop 'along their own lines' in their own areas. While they were in the 'white man's territory' (the whole of South Africa except for 13 per cent allocated as native reserves) they would be treated as migrants. 'The process of detribalisation,' it was stated, 'should be arrested.' At first sight, amid the clamour of the election, it might seem that this was little more than an elaboration of the old election cry, dear to audiences in the backveld, of *'die kaffir op sy plek en die koelie uit die land'* ('keep the black man in his place and send the Indian back to where he came from'); the difference, often overlooked at the time, was one of eventual aims: there were rigorous theoreticians who looked forward to the total transformation of South African society.

As an election slogan, apartheid had the advantage of promising firm but indefinite action to 'solve the native question' as distinct from the *laisser aller* attitude of the United Party. It was also, at that stage, vague enough to make it difficult to attack in detail, and those who questioned its premise could be dismissed as 'liberalists', *'kaffir-boeties'* (nigger-lovers), or advocates of race suicide. In the event, it is impossible to say exactly how much it had to do with the Nationalists' victory, or how many of those who voted for Malan had a clear idea of just what kind of mandate he was claiming. Apartheid was one of many election appeals. On the other side, the United Party offered the towering figure of Smuts, its war record, and the concepts of the 1930s. On the 'native question', they said that they recognised racial differences, repudiated equality, and talked of trusteeship and the development of the African under European guidance: this was the familiar language of the guardian and the ward, although nothing was said about when the ward would grow up. In short, the United Party scarcely recognised the changing tides of world opinion. The National Party did — and promised to swim against them.

In the general election of 1948, the Nationalists won 70 seats and their allies, the Afrikaner Party (the rump of the old Hertzogites), another 9. Between them, these parties had 40 per cent of the popular vote. Smuts and his allies, with a clear majority of the electorate, had 74 seats. Malan's majority was 5, slender but sufficient. Smuts himself was defeated in Standerton, and was returned to parliament in a seat vacated for him by one of his supporters.

A triumph for Afrikanerdom

It is easy in hindsight to misplace the incidence of the 1948 election. When its consequences became apparent later, it could be seen to have produced a constitutional revolution – a change in the political leadership, a change in the administrative elite, and a profound change in the philosophy and purpose of government. The immediate effects were not felt by the non-whites; that would come later, but for the moment they might feel that they had enjoyed little and been promised less. For the South African English, the shock was stunning and immediate. As a group, they had not been distinguished for political activity. Theirs had been the world of commerce and industry, and especially of mining and the professions. For years the Nationalists had taunted them with the reproach that they still regarded themselves as English rather than truly South African, that many of them knew little Afrikaans, were scornful of Afrikaner traditions and regarded the United Kingdom as 'home'. There was a half-truth in this, although many of the South African English knew little more of the country of their ancestors than the urbanised Africans of the Witwatersrand did of the remote traditions of their own tribes. Certainly, they had shown political complacency, content to shelter beneath the stature of Smuts. Now, for the first time, they experienced a total exclusion from political power at the national level. For the first time since union, the cabinet contained no person of English origin.

The Nationalists were exultant in victory; their country was now their own indeed. Many of them felt that the mills of God were grinding small at last: the republic was in sight, and the verdict of the Boer War could be reversed. The high places of politics had been captured; now was the time to make them secure, to consolidate success, to reward friends and settle old scores. There was something like a purge in the senior positions of the civil service, the armed forces and the police. Nationalist officers who had resigned their commissions at the out-

Left: General Smuts – happiest on the world stage – was oblivious to apartheid's growing appeal. In 1948 he paid the price

75

break of war found themselves reinstated, sometimes with back-dated promotion. There was an insistence on the use of Afrikaans in public offices, to the detriment of those who were deemed to be insufficiently bilingual. Some municipalities changed English street names, and switched their banking accounts to Afrikaner institutions. The military establishment at Roberts Heights, near Pretoria, was rechristened Voortrekkerhoogte. The non-nationalist Afrikaner often suffered both politically and socially for being a renegade from the *volk*.

The symbolic meaning was clear: wherever possible, purely sentimental links with England were to be broken. The immigration scheme introduced by the United Party was dismantled, and it was made more difficult for British subjects to acquire South African citizenship. The episode of the Uitlanders was not to be repeated. The parliamentary opposition pointed out the inconsistency between the claims of the Nationalists to be the protectors of 'white civilisation' and the measures which they were taking to make South Africa a harder place in which to settle. This missed the point that the phrase 'white civilisation' referred, first and foremost, to the specifically Afrikaner way of life—Calvinist, racial, and exclusive. The Nationalists and their opponents were speaking, literally and figuratively, different languages. To the Nationalists, arguments based on the premise of liberal individualism embodied a political heresy. What they were concerned with was the organic life of the group. And, as they had put it in an election manifesto: 'The State will exercise complete supervision over the moulding of the youth. The party will not tolerate interference from without or destructive propaganda from the outside world in regard to the racial problems of South Africa.'

The *laager* mentality and the mystique of the *volk*

It is important, for an understanding of the South African situation, to understand the essential characteristics of the kind of government which the Nationalists were bringing into being. It was inevitable, considering the times, that comparison should be made with Fascism, and some who should have known better were ready to compare Malan with Hitler. Superficial generalisations of this kind were wide of the mark, and darkened counsel. It would be more accurate to say that South Africa was governed by parliamentary authoritarianism. The Nationalists claimed to be democrats, but theirs was what Professor J.L.Talmon has called 'messianic democracy', something very different from the pragmatic rule of the representatives of a shifting and unstable majority. It was grounded upon a dogmatic assertion—that God had

endowed each 'nation' with a particular identity and purpose which could be discovered and achieved. Politics was a means of achieving this destiny; thus, it could not be separated from other aspects of life, nor confined within separate segments of activity. The devoted Nationalist (like the devoted Communist) could not say, with Henry V's army, 'We are but warriors for the working day'.

There was a qualitative difference between the Nationalists and the bulk of their opponents (with the exception of the small and ineffective Communist Party). The United Party and its allies were loose organisations, open to anyone who was prepared to indicate agreement with their general principles. They did not claim to exercise any general supervision over the conduct of their members, and they took for granted the fact that there existed a variety of activities which were altogether beyond the scope of direct political concern. By contrast, the doctrines of Afrikanerdom rested upon three props—Calvinist theology as interpreted by the Dutch Reformed churches; the idea of *taal en kultuur* (language and culture); and the National Party. A 'good Afrikaner' could not put on or take off his party obligations like a coat—they were regarded as an essential part of his identity. In practice, these obligations showed themselves in a pressure towards conformity.

The mythology of Afrikanerdom had been grounded on the memory of oppression. The characteristic posture in which the Afrikaner was portrayed by his leaders was one of wary defence, and the symbol of the *volk* might well be the *laager,* the protective waggon circle of the Voortrekkers. The dominating fact of South African history, as portrayed in Nationalist schools, had been the oppression of the Afrikaner by 'British imperialism'. Despite his victory in 1948, he was still, he felt, in danger—from 'foreign elements' which might corrupt his culture, from the 'money power' which might corrupt his soul, from doctrines of equality or liberalism or materialism, or just from the temper of the times. Behind all this, there was the threat from the black man. But the Afrikaner was confident of his ability to deal with that, provided that he was left alone and remained in power. There would be time to deal with the mythical empire of Prester John after he had dealt with the relics of the empire of Queen Victoria.

Thus, to the Afrikaner, the great question that had been settled in 1948 was the place of the Englishman in the political process. He had no place, so far as the ultimate decisions were concerned, except in so far as he was prepared to transform himself into a member of the *volk.*

Left: White South African troops—at one moment hailed as guardians of the free world, at the next a force for oppression

Apartheid in practice

Apartheid showed itself, immediately after 1948, in its most negative and protective sense. Legislation was passed to prohibit mixed marriages, and to extend the penalties for sexual intercourse across colour lines. A population register was created, in which men and women would be classified, in perpetuity, by race: there would be no more 'passing for white'. The Group Areas Act empowered the government, by administrative action, to enforce residential segregation in towns, not merely between whites and non-whites but between different kinds of non-whites as well. Certain areas had been set aside by the Native Land Act of 1913 exclusively for African occupation. By the end of the Second World War the area so reserved amounted to about 13 per cent of the area of the Union. There was an insistence upon what was called 'petty apartheid' – enforced separation in public places, in the use of public transport, lifts, lavatories, and entrances to public buildings. The promised positive side of apartheid was slow to appear. The Nationalists could claim that they were awaiting the reports of a series of committees, such as those on primary and secondary education, on the universities, and on the development of the native reserves (called, after their chairmen, the Eiselen, Holloway, and Tomlinson commissions). In the meantime, the country was distracted for five years by the constitutional conflict over the attempt by the government to remove the Coloured voters of the Cape Province from the common electoral roll.

This quarrel turned less upon the rights of the Coloured people than upon two interpretations of parliamentary government: did parliament represent an institution embodying the will of the electoral majority, and with unlimited powers of government; or were there certain limitations upon what a government might do? In essence, it was an ideological debate, of the greatest acrimony, between whites. The Act of Union of 1909, which laid down that voting rights might not be diminished except by a two-thirds majority of both Houses of Parliament in joint session, had been passed by the Parliament at Westminster. The principle involved had been part of the 'compact of union', and had represented a compromise between 'Cape liberalism' and the colour consciousness of the former republics. It was a reminder that apartheid, portrayed by its apologists as a logical extension of segregation, was only one among several 'South African traditions'. On the strictly legal side, there was a division of opinion whether, since the passing of the Statute of Westminster in 1931 and the explicit repeal of the Colonial Laws Validity Act of 1865, an imperial act was still

78

binding upon a dominion and whether, therefore, the entrenched clauses were still protected. The question, then, could be argued either morally or legally. The Nationalists took the view that the disputed clauses could be amended by simple majorities in either House: the parliament of South Africa was sovereign and could be bound by no higher authority. The long debate involved the nature of parliament, the place of the courts in the process of government, and—in the background—the status of English as an official language. The South Africa Act had laid down that Dutch (or Afrikaans, by later addition) and English were to be equally entrenched. But if one entrenched clause could be amended, why not another? In short, by what kind of a white majority should South Africa be governed—by a members' majority in parliament, or an electoral majority in the country as a whole? The Nationalists had a parliamentary majority which fell short of two-thirds. They were still a minority of the electorate.

The dying hopes of the United Party

The Act was passed by simple majorities in each House. It was then declared beyond the jurisdiction of the constitution by the Supreme Court, since it had not been passed by the procedure laid down in the South Africa Act. The issue then shifted to the place of the courts of law in the process of government. The Nationalists announced that it could not be permitted that judges should thwart the will of the people. The government passed an ill-digested statute setting up a 'high court of parliament' to be the final source of appeal in constitutional matters. The Supreme Court declared this body incompetent, since it was not a court in any meaningful sense of the word. It seemed that deadlock had been reached.

The constitutional crisis was the occasion for the emergence of an extra-parliamentary pressure group, the war veterans' Torch Commando. Its titular leader was Group-Captain 'Sailor' Malan, a hero of the Battle of Britain, and at its height it claimed a membership of more than 100,000. The avowed aim of the group was the 'preservation of the constitution'. It recaptured something of the camaraderie of the war, and canalised the resentment felt by the South African English and the Afrikaner supporters of Smuts against the tone and content of Nationalist government. It was concerned only indirectly with the question of colour, and made its stand on the terms of the Act of Union. There were embarrassed internal debates

Left: Torchlight procession in Cape Town—part of the protest against the government's apparently unconstitutional actions

within the Torch on whether Coloured ex-servicemen should be admitted to membership. It was decided that they should have separate branches of their own. The Torch held impressive parades. From time to time there were brawls with Nationalist supporters. The Afrikaans press could point out that the atmosphere of the early 1940s was being recreated, with the Torch taking the role of the *Ossewa Brandwag*. The Torch Commando generated internal enthusiasm, but made few converts. In the event, it had no permanent effect. It bent its energies to canvassing for the general election called for 1953, and it became, as it were, an extra-mural branch of the United Party.

The United Party looked forward hopefully to the election. There was a disposition to believe that the result of 1948 had been in some way accidental, and represented not the considered will of the electorate but the consequence of a protest vote by United Party supporters who now, after a taste of Nationalist rule, would return to their previous allegiance. In the meantime, the Nationalists had increased their majority by capturing all six seats newly allocated to the mandated territory of South-West Africa. However, opinion in this former German colony was not thought to be representative of that in the country at large. The result of the election came as a bewildering blow to the opposition. The Nationalists won 94 out of 156 seats, with an estimated 46 per cent of the total vote. The Afrikaner Party vanished, merged with the Nationalists. For the first time since Union, political power rested in a monolithic party, not in a coalition. In the election of 1953 the opposition had exerted all the effort of which it was capable, and that was not enough. It became clear that 1948 had not been merely an untoward event, but represented a permanent shift of power. Given the demographic trend, there would be proportionately more Afrikaners of voting age with each succeeding year. Hence, if a change were to come, it would have to be through a split in the Nationalist Party. This, it was quickly seen, was a forlorn hope. What splits there were came on the other side. The right wing of the United Party began to crumble and drift towards the Nationalists.

Left: Police strongarm tactics break up a women's meeting in the African location of Cato Manor. The meeting condemned the management of municipal beer halls and the brewing laws

Chapter 5

Apartheid and the Congress Movement

The battle over the constitution had been an episode in white politics. The issue affected only a fraction of the non-white people and even these, the Coloureds of the Cape Province, tended to regard the controversy with a certain fatalistic detachment. The non-whites of South Africa were not a community, but a set of groups and tribes, without a common language, at different stages of development, divided by ethnic hostilities and economic jealousies. In 1946, when Smuts was still in power, the Natal Indian Congress had attempted passive resistance against the Land Tenure Act, and had refused to co-operate in the election of white representatives to parliament. The attempt was a failure, and the election of 1948 changed the situation to the Indians' disadvantage. The United Party had offered them a fraction of a loaf, while the Nationalists were in no mood to offer anything at all. The offer of communal representation was withdrawn, and the Indians were left with no recourse but endurance of their lot or appealing to the government of India – a manoeuvre which produced no effect upon their condition and diminished what sympathy they had among the whites of Natal. The South African issue was kept alive at the United Nations, and the hostility generated there, if anything, helped to consolidate support for the Nationalist government at home.

The weakness of the Indians' position was shown with grim clarity in 1949, when there were serious racial riots in Durban. The immediate cause was trivial enough: an Indian storekeeper was said to have struck an African child, but the incident brought to the surface the smouldering enmity between Indians and Zulus. Durban experienced murder, arson, and looting, Indians were hunted through the streets, and the police opened fire to protect non-whites from each other. One lesson of the riots was that, in racial terms, the Indians seemed to be utterly friendless. The episode shocked the moderate leadership, and Indians and Africans managed some kind

Left: A gathering of Africans in Freedom Square, Johannesburg, demonstrates against the government's segregation measures

of rapprochement. This effort at co-operation was extended beyond the boundaries of Natal, and gave a new impetus to the African National Congress. This was a diffused and inchoate body, weak in organisation, with no mass support. It depended for its effectiveness upon the energy of individuals. Since the war, new men had been coming to the fore, thrusting out the older, more deferential leaders. The person whom they chose to represent them was Albert Luthuli, a former teacher and minor chief from Natal (who later won a Nobel peace prize). He was deprived of his chieftainship by the government after his election.

The resurgence of African political activity coincided roughly with the appointment, in 1950, of Hendrik Verwoerd as Minister of Native Affairs, and a consequent acceleration of the tempo of legislative and administrative activity in matters specifically affecting the Bantu-speaking population. The most significant sign of the new momentum was the passing of the Bantu Authorities Act of 1951, attacked by its opponents as an attempted reversion to a vanished tribalism, justified by Verwoerd as the first step towards the 'positive apartheid' which would provide a distinctive and separate communal life for the African. The Act abolished the Native Representative Council of 1936 and there were few to mourn its passing. In its place, the government sought to produce a form of indirect rule, based upon the authority of tribal chiefs, at the base; above the tribal councils would be a regional council, and above that a territorial council which might, in the future, look forward to some kind of autonomy. The weakness of the Act, in the eyes of its opponents, was that it took no account of the Africans in the towns. It was also argued that it sought to restore an irrecoverable past.

The Bantu Authorities Act was one of the six grievances put forward by the African National Congress in 1951, when it met in Bloemfontein, and passed resolutions calling upon the government to repeal, by February 1952, that Act, the pass laws, and the laws compelling the thinning out of stock in the reserves, the Group Areas Act, the Separate Representation of Voters Act, and the Suppression of Communism Act of 1950.

This action was the prelude to the 'defiance campaign' of 1952. It was significant that the African National Congress did not then make a specific demand for majority rule; they asked the government to move in the direction of a non-racial society. They announced their intentions in a letter to the Prime Minister, to which he replied in detail, rejecting their premises. Dr Malan took his stand upon the foundation stone of apartheid — the assertion that there were ineradicable differences between

Left: A Torch rally calls on the Malan government to resign

85

human beings. It was, he wrote, 'self-contradictory to claim as an inherent right of the Bantu, who differ in many ways from the Europeans, that they should be regarded as not different, especially when it is borne in mind that these differences are permanent and not man-made'. Culture, in other words, was inseparable from race. He went further, in an oblique reference to the gap between the elite of the African National Congress and the African masses, by claiming that laws were made for the good of the governed. 'Even those laws which are regarded as particularly irksome by the Bantu people have not been made in order to persecute them, but for the purpose of training them in the performance of those duties which must be fully observed by all those who wish to claim rights.'

The African National Congress and its allies were hoping to draw some white support; the beginning of their threatened campaign of passive resistance was deferred until the ending of the tercentenary celebrations of the landing of van Riebeeck at the Cape in 1652, lest sympathy be lost. In the event, very little sympathy was forthcoming. This was hardly surprising: the enemy of the white opposition was Afrikaner Nationalism, that of the Congress movement the whole structure of white supremacy, and European support for this structure was, in effect, unanimous. Malan was not quite accurate when he claimed that the essential point of conflict between whites was on the timing and method of legislation affecting non-whites. The crux of white politics was by which group of whites South Africa should be governed. As yet, less than half the electorate voted Nationalist but only a tiny fraction of the opposition was prepared to make common cause with non-whites, and it was comparatively easy for the government to claim that those were either Communists or their dupes.

The passive resistance campaign lasted from June until October in 1952. The lead was taken by Africans, but the ethos of the movement—the emphasis on non-violence, self-discipline, and willing acceptance of the consequences—owed much to Indian influence. In five months, about 8,500 volunteers were convicted for such offences as using amenities in public places reserved for whites only. The leaders were, for the most part, charged under

*Right: 1952 was the year of defiance. Indians march through Boksburg location in support of an African defiance group. Their own arrests soon followed. **Far right:** Albert Luthuli, advocate of non-violence and President of the African National Congress before its banning **(top)**; Patrick Duncan, son of a Governor-General of South Africa, and Manilal Gandhi, son of the Mahatma, together defy the permit regulations **(bottom)***

DRUM
africa's leading magazine
DECEMBER 1961 7½c

MY PLANS
by
A. J. LUTULI

a section of the Suppression of Communism Act which made it an offence to attempt to bring about political change by illegal action. This 'statutory Communism', as a judge described it, had nothing to do with Communism in the usual sense of the word.

The passive resisters were not seeking to coerce the State but to induce a change of mind on the part of the governors. Such a form of political activity can be successful only in certain conditions—if, for instance, it draws attention to an admitted grievance which has been neglected in the course of the political process. It may succeed if it can appeal to a divided mind, or causes persons not directly affected to change their political allegiance, or recruits effective support from some new source. Even then, it is probably necessary that what the governors are being asked to concede is not regarded by them as something necessary to salvation, in political, economic, or religious terms.

None of these conditions applied in South Africa. What was being asked for was not merely a reversal of the policy of apartheid, as a specifically Nationalist ideology, but the creation of a colour-blind society. The demeanour of the volunteers, in the first stages of the campaign, won them publicity abroad. This may have fortified their own resolution, but it did nothing to change the mind of the government. Once the movement led, however indirectly, to open violence, the government found itself supported by the official opposition in the maintenance of law and order. In October and November, there were riots in Port Elizabeth, East London, Kimberley, and on the Witwatersrand. In all these, the temper of the African mobs was indiscriminately hostile to whites. In all of them, the police opened fire. The episode which most shocked public opinion occurred at East London, with the murder and mutilation of a white nun who had acted as a missionary doctor in an African township. The campaign came to a sudden end.

There was one last gesture in December, when Patrick Duncan, the son of a former Governor-General, and Manilal Gandhi, the son of the Mahatma, committed the technical offence of entering an African township without a permit, and were arrested and sentenced. This was a token offer of support, and drew no imitators. When Parliament met in 1953, two laws—the Public Safety Act and the Criminal Laws Amendment Act—empowered the declaration of a state of emergency and enumerated heavy

Top right: Johannesburg protest meeting. **Bottom:** *Police charge a crowd of garment workers demonstrating against the arrest under the Suppression of Communism Act of their union secretary, E.L.Sachs, after a strike involving 18,000 workers in 1952*

penalties for those who broke the law by way of political protest. The United Party, with an eye on the coming election, voted for both measures.

This episode illuminated the dilemma of the United Party, now drifting slowly with the tide, after the death in 1950 both of Jan Hofmeyr and General Smuts. The party was essentially one of coalition, founded on the consensus of 1934. It did not possess a distinctive doctrine, and professed equal respect for the rights of English and Afrikaner. It was a party of organisation rather than ideology, including men and women of all shades of non-Nationalist opinion. Since the break with Hertzog in 1939, the unifying element in the party had been the figure of Smuts.

Smuts's successor, Jacobus Strauss, did not command the same charismatic devotion. As the United Party viewed the situation, the foremost task was to defeat the Nationalist Party at the polls, and to do this it would have to cut deeply into the Afrikaner vote. It continued to hope that it would attract the 'moderate Nationalist' who might be repelled by the rigorousness of the government, and its breaking of the familiar ties with the past. It was particularly sensitive to accusations that it was 'soft on Communism' or that its policies might endanger white supremacy. It had a hard conservative core.

After 1948, its right-wing had found a scapegoat for defeat in the 'liberalism' of Jan Hofmeyr. It was now showing signs of strain. After 1953, six of its members broke away to form the Conservative Party, which sought for some compromise with the Nationalists on the constitutional issue. On the non-Communist left, the party lost potential support through the formation, in 1953, of the South African Liberal Party. This stood for an open society and a colour-blind franchise, and found spokesmen in Parliament in the native representatives. It attracted support in the English universities, and it had non-white members. Its greatest importance, perhaps, was its indication that the United Party was no longer the focal point of opposition.

The political credo of Daniel Malan

In 1954 Malan retired; he was eighty years old. There were good reasons why he should be regarded as the Moses of his people, the man who had led them, with remarkable consistency, towards the Promised Land. He was an essentially conservative figure, and his vision of

Left: An outbreak of pass burning swept South Africa in 1952. These 'passes' restricting the freedom of movement of Africans were resented as badges of inferiority. They had to be carried at all times: failure to produce them was a criminal offence

apartheid did not encompass the more extensive hopes of some of his younger followers. He had rejected complete territorial separation as impossible. It would, he said in 1950, be an 'ideal state' if it could be achieved, but it was impracticable in a country where the economic structure was based on native labour. He had been wary of formulating a precise definition of apartheid. It was not, he insisted, a policy of oppression. 'On the contrary, like a wire fence between two neighbouring farms, it indicates a separation without eliminating necessarily legitimate and desirable contacts in both directions, and although it places reciprocal restrictions on both sides, it, at the same time, serves as an effective protection against violation of one another's rights.' It could be argued that this postulated a static society, or at least one in which non-white aspirations could be controlled 'objectively' by white men. In February 1954, Malan set out the foundations of his policy with remarkable candour in a letter to the Reverend J.E.Piersman, an American divine. 'The deep-rooted colour consciousness of the white South Africans—a phenomenon quite beyond the comprehension of the uninformed—arises from the fundamental differences between the two groups, white and black. The difference in colour is merely the physical manifestation of the contrast between two irreconcilable ways of life, between barbarism and civilisation, between heathenism and Christianity, and finally between overwhelming numerical odds on the one hand and insignificant numbers on the other . . . Small wonder that the instinct of self-preservation is so inherent in the white South African. He has retained his identity all these years. He is not willing to surrender it now.'

It was no secret that Malan would have liked to have been succeeded by Nicolaas Havenga, once the principal confidant of General Hertzog, but Havenga had no personal following. The party caucus chose Johannes Strijdom of the Transvaal, 'the Lion of the North', who had been associated with the most intransigent wing of the party. This was an indication that the Nationalist centre of gravity had shifted from the Cape. The accession of Strijdom meant, among other things, a significant increase in the power of Verwoerd. Apartheid, to Malan, had been a distant ideal—to Verwoerd, it was something which would be made to work.

Since 1953 there had been an armistice in the battle of the constitution. Strijdom resumed the conflict. The Coloured vote was entrenched in the constitution, but the composition of the Senate, the upper house, was not.

Left: *Police, equipped with powers of summary arrest, make a random swoop to check on offences against the pass laws*

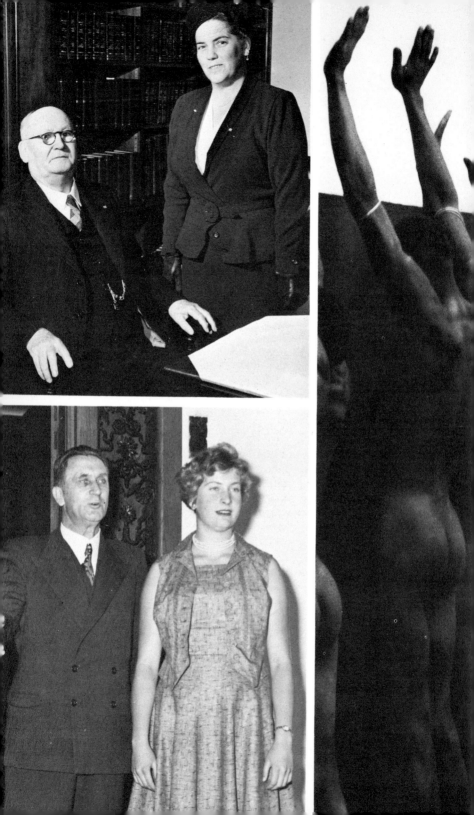

Strijdom proposed to enlarge the Senate in such a way as to give his government the necessary two-thirds majority. The second phase of the crisis lasted throughout 1955 and 1956. It provoked more manifestations of opposition outside parliament, but it was clear that the tempo of protest was slackening. An attempt was made to resurrect the Torch Commando, but that organisation was found to be dead beyond recall. The most spectacular of the new movements was the Women's Defence of the Constitution League, later called the Black Sash. This again was essentially a form of passive protest, an appeal to the conscience of the governors. Members of the Black Sash—European women of the upper middle classes—took to the 'haunting' of cabinet ministers. Wearing sashes of mourning, and displaying the slogan *Eerbiedig Ons Grondwet* (honour and respect our constitution), they positioned themselves on public occasions in such a way that ministers were forced to pass between a double line of mourners. The reaction to the Senate Bill produced other and shorter-lived organisations, such as the Covenant Movement and the Anti-Republican League. All these were at pains to repudiate any connection with the United Party. In part, this was a tactical decision: the target was still the 'moderate Nationalist' who might be stirred by what was a clear repudiation of the spirit of the compromise of union. There was a brief flurry of excitement when thirteen Afrikaner academics from Pretoria signed a public letter of protest against the Senate Bill. Their example was not followed by the majority of Afrikaners, and some of them paid the penalty of social ostracism. But it could be said that the actions of the government were producing, by way of reaction, a certain amount of rethinking on the part of some whites on the issue of colour.

The dilemma inherent in this new attitude could be seen in the fortunes and deliberations of the newly-formed Liberal Party. Like other parties of that persuasion, the Liberals faced the difficulty of combining an appeal to the bourgeois virtues of their creed with an appeal to the masses. It showed itself in the protracted debate about whether the party should stand for a qualified franchise or for universal suffrage. In one sense, the debate was unreal. The Liberals had no chance of gaining power from a white electorate, and the debate was therefore of an academic nature, concerned with the attitude to be taken in a hypothetical future situation.

Far left: Architects of segregation — D.F.Malan, Nationalist Prime Minister from 1948 to 1954 (top), and J.G.Strijdom, his successor (bottom). Left: Separate development did not stop the recruitment of unskilled African labour into the mines

95

What was important was to stand for the principle of multi-racialism. Others argued that this attitude was tantamount to adopting the slogan 'All power to the Africans'. The root of the problem lay in the white electorate, which must be convinced that there was a middle way between the stark alternatives posed by the Nationalists—race suicide or apartheid. Therefore, it must be demonstrated that moderate Africans would join a political party which offered them a share but not a monopoly of power. On the other side, it was argued that unless the Liberals adopted universal suffrage as a plank in their platform, they would not appeal to Africans, who would either move towards an exclusive nationalism of their own or else drift under the influence of Communists.

Communism: the black man's friend?

The Communist Party had been outlawed, but there were many organisations in which Communist influence was important. When it came to appealing to Africans, the Liberals had no rivals on their right, but they were under constant pressure to move to the left. So far as most Africans who thought about these matters were concerned, 'Communism' carried none of the ideological overtones which made the vast majority of white South Africans shrink instinctively from it. There were not many Maoists or Marxist-Leninists among the African intelligentsia, but there were many who were prepared to accept offers of help from any quarter. Communism was said to stand for racial equality: the Chinese were non-whites, and the Russians were said to be opposed to colonialism.

The Suppression of Communism Act had produced one unexpected result—it had enabled some Communists to break through the crust of suspicion, hardening into hatred, which divided white and black in the cities. It was very hard indeed for whites to know just what Africans were thinking. The old-style Afrikaner had always claimed that he properly understood the African mind—what was required was firmness, which was instinctively respected. There was a half-truth in this contention. Some Africans were of the opinion that 'you know where you are with the Dutchman'. There, the enemy was clearly in sight: he might be hated or feared, but he might also be accorded some of the respect which he claimed to possess. The African stereotype of the South African English was of a creature more baffling. Anthony Sampson, a journalist from England who edited an African magazine, quoted a black man who said to him: 'I hate you Liberals. I can't hate the others because I don't meet them.' However pure the intentions of the white Liberals, their very circumstances made it hard for them

to meet Africans on terms of equality. African and Communist could possess a certain comradeship in persecution: 'the enemy of my enemy is my friend'.

The government achieved a considerable success in 1955, when the Transkeian Territories General Council, an African consultative body of the Xhosa people, accepted the principle of the Bantu Authorities Act. One of the arguments used in justification of apartheid was that what the government claimed to be the inherent right of the white man – the preservation of his identity – could not be denied to other national groups. Thus, the government was committed to the stimulation of African nationalism. There was the obvious danger that such a movement would be hostile to the white man.

Two assumptions underlay the official policy: the African would want what the government required him to want, and he would be pacific in his actions. Certain of the chiefs had now been won over, but the African National Congress declared that it stood for a multi-racial, integrated society. The government's reply was that the Congress leadership was unrepresentative, that it did not understand what was in the best interests of their own people, and that it was led astray by agitators.

More and more, Dr Verwoerd was appearing as the 'legislator' of Rousseau's *Social Contract,* pointing out to Africans what their 'real will' ought to be. Unlike Rousseau's father-figure, however, the Minister of Native Affairs had behind him the sanction of force. In a literal manner, the African might be 'forced to be free'. Professor Edgar Brookes, formerly a senator, pointed the contradiction: the African would 'develop along his own lines', but a committee of white men would tell him what those lines were going to be.

The leadership of the African National Congress had been moderate enough, but it was under pressure to move towards militancy. What success, it was asked, had caution produced? The Congress leaders had, as it were, knocked politely at a door which remained firmly closed. The young lions of the 1940s – men like Nelson Mandela, Potlako Leballo, Oliver Tambo, and Robert Sobukwe – had now reached the age of authority. They were well-educated young men who, for the most part, represented a new and militant generation, not prepared, as their elders had been, to look forward indefinitely to the day when the whites should experience a charge of heart. They pressed for direct action, to produce some improvement in the political position of the Africans in their own lifetime. To these men, economic advancement, as a by-product of European development, was not **100** ▷

Left: Separate education for Africans – a makeshift schoolroom

The appeal of apartheid

South Africa's system of apartheid (which means literally 'separateness') is unparalleled in world history. Its apologists see it as the only practicable response to South Africa's unique historical status as both motherland and colony. South Africa's colonial peoples, lacking an ocean to divide them from their rulers, wanted a share in the government at Cape Town. The Afrikaner felt that his God-given national identity was at stake; the English resented the challenge to *baasskap* or white supremacy. So apartheid emerged as the tailor-made justification for the retention of power by a minority, with its African 'homelands' **(below)**, its rigid segregation of the races **(right)**, and its promise of self-government for Africans in their own areas at some indefinite future date. In practice the non-whites became trespassers in their own land, while drastic shortages of skilled labour threatened to make the system unworkable. Job reservation means widespread underemployment.

enough. Albert Luthuli, president of the Congress, was a man of massive simplicity and integrity, but behind him, in what came to be known as the Congress Alliance, were men of nimbler minds and more devious purposes. Some of them had acquired experience in China and the Soviet Union, and there had also been unofficial delegates from South Africa at the Bandung conference on Afro-Asian unity, of April 1955. (It was to prevent such contacts that the government, in 1955, made it a criminal offence to leave the country without a valid passport.)

In 1955 a 'Congress of the People' met near Johannesburg. There were nearly 3,000 delegates at this gathering, which was made up of representatives of the African National Congress, the South African Indian Congress, the National Union of the Organisation of Coloured People, and a white group with Communist affiliations which called itself the Congress of Democrats. The Congress endorsed a document known as the Freedom Charter, which combined its far-reaching hopes, and exhortations to peace and brotherly love, with certain specific demands—universal suffrage, the equal rights of 'all national groups and races', the nationalisation of banks, mines, and industry, the sharing of the land, and the abolition of apartheid in all its forms. The slogan 'The people shall govern' now began to make its appearance on hoardings and the walls of public buildings.

The government's reaction to the Congress of the People was to conduct an extended series of police raids on a number of organisations and individuals. At the end of 1956, it arrested about 150 men and women, of all races, and charged them with the common law crime of high treason. The trial dragged on for five years. For the defence was assembled what was probably the most eminent team of legal counsel ever to act in a South African trial. In 1961, the accused were acquitted. By then, however, the South African situation had drastically changed.

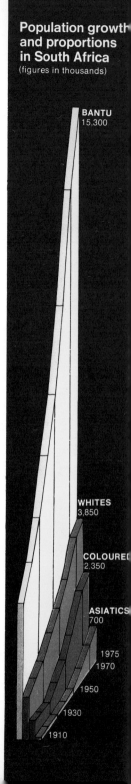

Population growth and proportions in South Africa
(figures in thousands)

BANTU
15,300

WHITES
3,850

COLOURED
2,350

ASIATICS
700

1975
1970
1950
1930
1910

Right: Diagrams showing the racial background to apartheid. By the year 2000 there will be 35 to 40 million blacks in South Africa, eight million Coloureds, two million Asians, and only six million whites. Only 13 per cent of South Africa's land area is reserved for the blacks: will it be enough?

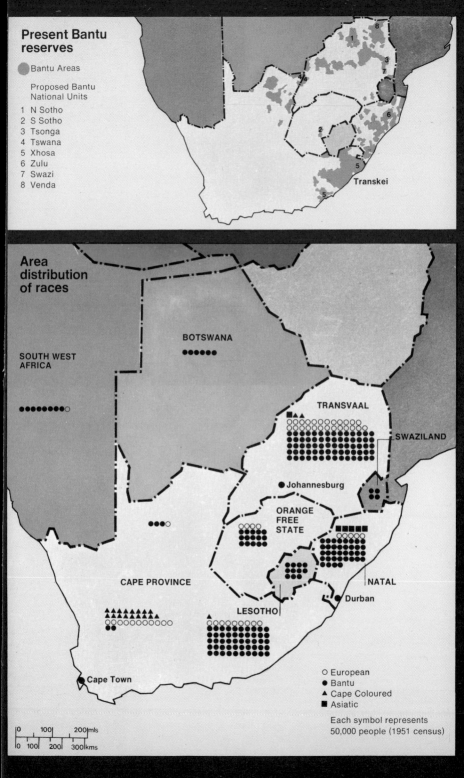

Present Bantu reserves

- Bantu Areas

Proposed Bantu National Units

1 N Sotho
2 S Sotho
3 Tsonga
4 Tswana
5 Xhosa
6 Zulu
7 Swazi
8 Venda

Transkei

Area distribution of races

SOUTH WEST AFRICA

BOTSWANA

TRANSVAAL

SWAZILAND

● Johannesburg

ORANGE FREE STATE

NATAL

CAPE PROVINCE

LESOTHO

● Durban

● Cape Town

○ European
● Bantu
▲ Cape Coloured
■ Asiatic

Each symbol represents 50,000 people (1951 census)

0   100   200 mls
0   100   200   300 kms

Chapter 6
Republicanism Regained

Johannes Strijdom died in office in 1958. There were three candidates for the succession, and for the first time the National Party formally balloted for its leader. Hertzog, Malan, and Strijdom had all, in their time, emerged. Verwoerd was elected. Those who saw in this contest a sign of internal strain among the Nationalists were disappointed. The election over, the party clicked into line. Verwoerd was, indeed, a messianic figure, with a different attitude to politics from the pragmatism and conservatism of his predecessors. He believed in two things with passionate intensity – the necessity, for South Africa, of achieving the status of a republic, and the possibility of apartheid being made to work. He had been born in Holland and had his first education in Rhodesia. He had studied psychology and sociology at the universities of Stellenbosch, Hamburg, Leipzig, and Berlin. His South Africanism had about it something of the fervour of the convert. He was a prodigious worker, convinced of the rightness of his own opinions, who quickly came to exercise an undisputed mastery over his party. It was doubtful whether he was ever a figure of affection, as Malan and Strijdom had been to their followers, but he was accorded a respect mixed with awe.

It might well seem, to the observer, that ten years of the policy of apartheid had achieved little but to sharpen hostilities within South Africa, and to make South Africa a target of unpopularity both for liberals in the West and Communists in the East. By 1958, the South African population exceeded 14,000,000 – 3,000,000 whites, nearly 10,000,000 Africans, nearly 500,000 Indians, and about 1,400,000 Coloureds. In spite of the rigour of the pass laws, and attempts to enforce limitation on the flow of non-whites into the urban areas, twelve of the thirteen largest towns had substantial non-white majorities. Only Pretoria could still claim to have an overall white majority. The Tomlinson Commission had reported discouragingly on the prospect of territorial separation. It was just not

Left: Midnight celebrators in Pretoria greet the news that South Africa has left the Commonwealth and become a republic

103

possible to shift the African population, in any fore-
seeable future, into the reserves. The crux of the problem
remained where it had been all through the century – in
the towns.

Considerable pressure was being put upon the South
African government, by the older dominions, by the
United Kingdom, and by the United States, to make some
concessions which might mitigate hostility at the United
Nations and relieve the strains within the Commonwealth posed by the presence of South Africa in what
was becoming an organisation no longer dominated by the
older white dominions. Trade boycotts were attempted,
and there were efforts to induce the United Nations to
apply economic sanctions. For the moment, these activities
had little practical effect. The countries which had the
power to damage South Africa had no desire to do so,
and those which clamoured most loudly for forceful intervention did not possess the means. The status of South-
West Africa, mandated to South Africa after the First
World War, was to be tested in a case before the World
Court, brought by Liberia and Ethiopia.

Verwoerd's political aims

Verwoerd's reaction to pressure from without was to
move swiftly, not in the direction of multi-racialism but
towards more extreme political apartheid. In 1959 he
pushed through Parliament the Promotion of Bantu
Self-Government Act, which envisaged the creation of
eight 'national units' for the African people. He enunci-
ated three principles: God had a divine purpose for every
people, irrespective of race or colour; every people had
an inherent right of existence and of self-government;
personal, no less than national, aspirations should be
fulfilled within one's own community. He talked of an
eventual commonwealth of South African states, black
and white. Where Malan had said that territorial separation was impracticable, Verwoerd declared that, if faced
with the alternative of a small white state or a larger one
that was multi-racial, he would choose the smaller.

Early in 1960, he announced that a referendum would
be held later that year, in which white voters would
choose whether South Africa should become, immediately,
a republic within the Commonwealth. This, too, was a
new departure. His predecessors had been content to

Top right: C.R.Swart, first President of the new republic, ad-
dressing the crowd. Dr Verwoerd, Prime Minister since 1958,
listens on the left. *Bottom:* Swart's Cabinet reads like a roll-
call of Afrikanerdom. Albert Hertzog, son of the former Prime
Minister, who later founded the extreme right-wing break-
away Reformed National Party, is on the far right, back row

shelve this issue until the anti-republican South African English had become converted. Verwoerd was prepared to force the issue at once, and induce the opponents of the republic to become converted after the event.

The two issues were, indeed, closely connected. Verwoerd was moving faster than any previous leader of the *volk*. He was proposing to bring apartheid down from the clouds of theory into the realities of administration – to graft on the practice of racial segregation the immediate granting of certain political powers, however limited, to Africans. He spoke the language of sacrifice: the white South African would have to pay a certain price for his privileged position. He could not have it both ways, enjoy both affluence and security, retain the African as labourer and servant and simultaneously be secure against the political pretensions of a black proletariat. Political apartheid, it was strongly suggested, might be only the first step. The partition of South Africa might one day become a reality. In the meantime, Verwoerd's critics pointed out, 'political apartheid' was no answer to the problem of the growing African majorities in the cities. There, answered Verwoerd, the African would remain without political rights. This, he claimed, was parity of treatment, because the European would, similarly, have no rights in African areas. But, it could be argued, there was no imperative necessity for the European to go to an African area to earn his subsistence, while the Africans in the reserves, as a whole, could maintain themselves only by the product of migrant labour. There was constant reiteration of the prophecy that some time in the future – the year 1978 was repeatedly mentioned – the movement of population would change direction, and a term would be set to the growth of the urban African population. But, it could be contended, the process of bringing about even a limited form of apartheid, was enormously increasing the tensions across the colour line which it was the avowed intention of apartheid to eliminate.

South Africa becomes a republic
There were conservative Afrikaners who considered that Verwoerd was moving too fast. To men of this persuasion, there was held out the promise of the republic, an issue which was calculated to unite Nationalists as nothing else could. The referendum was conducted on the premise that a republic of South Africa would be admitted, on the precedent set by India, to continued membership of the Commonwealth. In October 1960, Verwoerd gained a majority of 70,000 for the republic out of a total of 1,600,000 votes cast. He had argued

Right: *Sowing dragons' teeth – a cartoonist's sardonic comment*

106

his case on the assertion that only the coming of the republic would end the strife between white South Africans; until then, the nationalist would not be satisfied, and the South African English would not bring themselves to an undivided loyalty.

Verwoerd was not a professional psychologist for nothing. His personal appeal, sent out in a facsimile of his own handwriting in a letter to voters in both official languages, and beginning 'Dear Friend', contrived to associate the idea of the monarchy with the forces prepared to sacrifice the white man for the appeasement of African nationalism. 'The struggle between Eastern and Western nations, between Communism and Christendom, is such that both groups of nations will grant and concede anything (including the white man of Africa, his possessions, and his rights) to seek the favour and support of the black man. This has led to chaos in the Congo.' Hence, he argued, the necessity for the whites of South Africa to combine for their own protection. It was an old argument, with a new twist: appeals of this kind had, in the past, been made to the 'moderate Afrikaner'; now they were being directed at the 'moderate Englishman'.

In part, the envisaged creation of what came to be known as 'Bantustans' (a name coined, on the analogy of Pakistan, to denote a separate African area, with eventual self-government) was a reaction to the emergence of new African states. The independence of Ghana in 1957 had something of the fascination, to politically-conscious Africans, which President Kruger's republic had offered to the Cape Dutch in the 1890s. If Verwoerd had hoped that the promise of some form of political autonomy to the new territorial units would still the protests of South Africa's critics, he was disappointed. In a remarkable speech in Cape Town, Harold Macmillan, the British Prime Minister, spoke of the 'winds of change' blowing through Africa, and warned the South African government that it could no longer rely on British support, either in the Commonwealth or in the United Nations. South Africa, he said, very plainly, had become a political embarrassment to its former friends.

On the side of the non-whites, however, the brief unity of the Congress Movement had already begun to crumble. The Africans, like some of the whites, had begun to rethink their position, and some of them were beginning to advocate direct action. In its slow development, African nationalism had passed through various overlapping phases. The older generation of Congress leaders had not expected to achieve substantial rights in their own life-

Left: *The cramped quarters of a compound for African mine-workers contrast with the luxuriance of a Cape Dutch homestead*

109

times. They considered themselves as sowing seeds for the future, in the hope that the white man would change his attitude to Africans, once a substantial number of them had become educated. Men like John Tengo Jabavu, a cultivated moderate of the old-style African political leaders, had clung, at the time of union, to the hope that Cape liberalism would survive and grow. Salvation might eventually come to the Africans through individual contacts and friendships with whites, it was thought.

The early leaders of the National Native Congress assumed that the very fact of African unity would produce an extension of liberty. They were anxious not to arouse white suspicions by militancy or extravagant demands. They held meetings and passed resolutions, which were conveyed deferentially to those in authority. They did not take the initiative, but waited for the government to act, and then made dignified protests. There were others who thought, in the distant future, of a united front of Africans, who might recover the 'national spirit' of a quasi-mythical past. This attitude had been associated with the Reverend John Dube, who had been educated in the United States. 'Where once there was a pool,' he declaimed, 'water will collect again.' The African must break away from his tribal past, and infiltrate himself into European society. A few talked of open conflict, and of recovering their rights on the battlefield, but they were small in numbers and influence.

The Freedom Charter of 1955 had spoken the language of millenialism and was heavy with the overtones of Utopia. It in some way resembled the *cahiers* presented to the Estates-General of France in 1789. It made a series of demands, intended to redress past grievances. When taken together, these demands amounted to a total rejection of the existing political, economic, and social structure of South Africa. They could be summarised according to its chapter headings: 'The people shall govern. . . . All national groups shall have equal rights. . . . The people shall share the country's wealth. . . . The land shall be shared among those who work it. . . . All shall be equal before the law. . . . All shall enjoy equal human rights. . . . There shall be work and security. . . . The doors of learning and culture shall be opened. . . . There shall be houses, security, and comfort. . . . There shall be peace and friendship. . . .' There was no real hope that the Charter would ever be implemented as a political programme.

In the Congress Alliance, the African National Congress lost the advantages of its numbers. The initiative in the steering committee was held by the small but

Left: African women disperse after demonstrating in Cato Manor

influential group of Europeans from the Congress of Democrats. There were some Africans, such as Robert Sobukwe, who claimed that multi-racialism meant Communist control. He broke away to form the Pan-African Congress, exclusively nationalist and racialist. Where the Congress of Democrats looked to the East, the Pan-Africanists looked to the North for their allies—particularly to the ranging ambitions of Dr Nkrumah of Ghana.

The tragedy of Sharpeville

It was the internal conflict between the two wings of the African movement that gave rise to the tragic events at Sharpeville in 1960. In December 1959, the African National Congress called for a demonstration against the pass laws, to be held on 31st March 1960. The Pan-Africanists called for demonstrations of their own, ten days earlier. Africans were encouraged to burn or surrender their passes; it was believed that the government would be forced to make concessions or to face a condition of chaos.

The background to these events was one of extreme tension. There had been a disastrous mining accident, costing many lives. In Natal, a squad of police carrying out a routine raid on an African township had been attacked, and some of them had been killed.

On 21st March, the Pan-Africanists' demonstrations took place. At Sharpeville, an African township in the Transvaal, the police opened fire with rifles and Stenguns, killing 69 Africans and wounding more than 150 others. This was an episode that shocked the world. Sharpeville passed into the mythology of horror stories. On the BBC, Richard Dimbleby made comparisons with Guernica and Lidice, the communities in Spain and Czechoslovakia destroyed by the Nazis. The analogy was grotesque, but it gave some indication of the wave of emotion generated by the event. In fact, Sharpeville was a disastrous accident, a likely product of a condition in which the police had long been encouraged to shoot when they considered themselves in danger. The controversy turned on whether the danger, on that day, had been real. There was no blinking the fact that the police had fired on an unarmed crowd.

In South Africa, it seemed that the threatened upheaval, so long evoked in fear or hope as a calamity, or as a means to a new condition of society, had come at last. The government declared a state of emergency, and arrested about 1,600 persons. For the first time, members of the Liberal Party found themselves in confinement. The Anglican Bishop of Johannesburg fled to Swaziland, and later made his way to England. His action was much criticised by members of his own communion, and the government met with comparatively little opposition

when it refused to allow him to return to the country. It seemed that violence was imminent when a great column of Africans from the outlying townships began to march towards Cape Town. In the event they were stopped by armed police, and dispersed—the fists clenched, but remaining in the pockets. On 9th April, an English farmer shot and wounded Verwoerd in the head as he was opening a trade fair in Johannesburg. It seemed that change by shock was coming to South Africa at last.

It did not happen. Sharpeville was the turning point at which no one turned. Verwoerd recovered, and his presence in hospital did not relax his complete and undivided control over the government. He made it plain that there would be no concessions in any direction, and that South Africa would go on as before. A new ruthlessness was now introduced into the process of government. The African National Congress and the Pan-Africanists were both banned. Sobukwe was tried and sentenced to a term of imprisonment. Thereafter he was kept in preventive detention for six years. African leaders were banished or placed under restriction. Verwoerd made it clear that he would not deviate either from the creation of Bantustans or from the republican referendum.

The African members of the Commonwealth were not prepared to forget Sharpeville. Verwoerd found himself confronted, at the conference of March 1961, with demands that the price of membership would be a change in the policy of apartheid. He withdrew his application for continued membership. On 31st May 1961, the fifty-ninth anniversary of the Peace of Vereeniging, South Africa became a republic, outside the Commonwealth and friendless, it seemed, except for the small white communities of Mozambique, Rhodesia, and Angola.

Once again, prophecies of disaster were unfulfilled. Indeed, it might seem that all political organisations in South Africa were splitting from within, except the National Party. The African organisations were prohibited and disrupted. The United Party had split in 1959, when its 'liberal' wing hived off to form the Progressive Party, which stood for a qualified franchise, a federal state, and a society based, as its slogan went, on 'merit not colour'. There was considerable enmity between the Progressives and their former colleagues of the United Party; they were not popular, either, with the Liberals. The general election of 1961 was a massive victory for the Nationalists. It showed a general swing to the right. The Progressives for the most part fought the United Party: they polled 70,000 votes in the constitu-

Left: About half a million Africans a year are arrested for offences under laws that apply only or principally to Africans

encies which they contested, but succeeded in electing only one of their candidates, Mrs Helen Suzman, in the rich Johannesburg seat of Houghton. Her supporters could claim, without preposterous exaggeration, that she effectively was the South African opposition.

Nothing, perhaps, was more remarkable about the career of Verwoerd than the manner in which, as his premiership continued, he gained the support of the South African English. In 1961 the Nationalists had won their fourth general election in succession. In political terms, it could be said that South Africa had developed into a hybrid state, with the formal structure of a multi-party system and the reality of single-party rule. Many of the South African English had become weary of the posture of protest. The clamorous hostility of the outside world made little differentiation between white South Africans. White South Africans tended to band together in resistance to a common enmity. Verwoerd offered them security. It was doubtful what other security could be found.

The tide was running strongly towards the Nationalists. The economy swiftly recovered from the shock of confidence of 1960 and 1961. The middle 1960s were boom years, and coincided with an outbreak of sabotage and violence. The African nationalist movements had gone underground. At the end of 1961, they announced the formation of the Spear of the Nation (an offshoot of the African National Congress) and Poqo, a terrorist group connected with the Pan-Africanists. There were attempts to blow up power lines. There were isolated and indiscriminate attacks upon whites. The government reacted with more severe legislation – sabotage became a capital offence, and the police were empowered to detain suspects for up to ninety days without trial. The Minister of Justice was empowered to impose a form of detention known as 'house arrest', by which men and women might be confined to their homes for specified periods. These activities were strongly criticised in the English press as violations of the rule of law, and the introduction of the methods of the police state. The government's reply was that the question was one of white survival: *Salus populi est suprema lex* (the welfare of the people is the highest law). A new and formidable figure had appeared in the person of Balthazar John Vorster, who made a reputation for unswerving sternness as Minister of Justice.

There remained isolated islands of opposition among the white community – in the English press, the English

Right: Aftermath of Sharpeville – the worst clash between Africans and police in South African history. It came to symbolise in the eyes of the world the relentless logic of apartheid

universities, and in the churches. The Black Sash continued its activities. Student movements continued to speak the language of the Declaration of Human Rights. In 1959, after a struggle lasting five years, the government had deprived the universities of Cape Town and the Witwatersrand of their right to admit non-white students, and had set up a number of non-white colleges. Both universities continued to stand for the principles of multi-racialism in higher education, but they were visibly losing support. In the 1950s protest marches in the streets of Johannesburg had been greeted with signs of sympathy. In the 1960s they evoked public hostility. White opinion was shocked by the revelations of the 'Rivonia trial' (named after the Johannesburg suburb in which the arrests were made), when the leaders of the resistance movements were convicted of offences under the sabotage laws, and sentenced to life imprisonment. A group of young white intellectuals attempted to continue the movement of sabotage, but there was a revulsion after one young man had exploded a petrol bomb in the crowded concourse of the Johannesburg station.

The government continued to press forward in two directions. It strengthened the apparatus of defence and coercion, took new powers for the police, introduced compulsory military service, and built up armaments. It also went forward with what had now come to be called 'separate development' and, in 1963, passed the Transkeian Constitution Act, setting up the first of the territorial authorities. A Xhosa chieftain, Kaiser Mantanzima, became the first chief minister of a 'Bantustan'. He owed his majority to a number of government-appointed chieftains, but it could be shown that there were Africans prepared to co-operate with the government.

The garrison state
The fifth anniversary of the republic, in 1966, was made the occasion for an impressive demonstration of the strength of the South African armed forces. Inside and outside South Africa, the government seemed immune from threats. Some African states continued to speak the language of war towards South Africa, but it could be shown that they had neither the resources nor the inner cohesion to do more than talk. Moreover, it could not be denied that the country was becoming richer, that the Africans were sharing, however disproportionately, in the general prosperity, and that the government's security forces were powerful enough to deal with any attempted revolt. In short, there was no revolutionary situation. The non-white masses were leaderless and subservient. Moreover, the South African government was receiving a measure of support from new

African states. The former protectorates of Bechuanaland, Basutoland, and Swaziland were granted independence; their governments made it clear that they wished to live at peace with their neighbour. To the north, the state of Malawi, under the lead of Dr Kamuzu Banda, refused to share in the general (and ineffective) gestures of boycotts and enmity.

On 6th September 1966, Verwoerd was stabbed to death on the floor of the House of Assembly. His killer was a parliamentary messenger named Tsafendas, who was found unfit to plead at his trial, and confined as a madman. The murder produced no political crisis: the National Party elected John Vorster to the leadership, and the country continued on its way.

It was widely believed that the election of Vorster would see an end to the politics of messianism, and a return to pragmatic opportunism. There was, certainly, a change in style, but no discernible change in direction. Political apartheid was carried a stage further by the effective prohibition of multi-racial political parties. The Liberal Party dissolved itself, the Progressives continued, shorn of their non-white members.

There were signs that the Nationalist Party was attempting to become less exclusive, and more prepared to offer a home to the converted Englishman. Verwoerd and Vorster both claimed to stand for white civilisation rather than the narrower concept of Afrikanerdom. In the middle 1960s, there were the beginnings of a serious ideological quarrel within the inner circles of Nationalism, between two groups who came to be known as the *verligtes* (the enlightened) and the *verkramptes* (the cramped conservatives). The quarrel turned on such matters as the attitude of South Africa to African states, the introduction of television, the policy to be adopted towards rugby matches against New Zealand teams containing Maoris and, in general, South Africa's attitude to the world at large. This was not a debate over the essentials of white supremacy. In it, Vorster could appear as a *verligte,* and his opponents were far to the right. There was no comfort in this quarrel for liberals or multi-racialists.

*Left: Political figures of South Africa. **Left-hand column from top:** John Vorster, Verwoerd's successor as Prime Minister; Alan Paton, internationally-known writer and member of the now banned Liberal Party; Harry Oppenheimer, millionaire industrialist and ex-United Party MP; Helen Suzman, the Progressives' lone MP. **Right-hand column:** Mantanzima, first chief of the Transkeian Bantustan; Nelson Mandela and Robert Sobukwe — African Nationalist leaders detained by the government; Sir de Villiers Graaff, the leader of the United Party*

Conclusion

After twenty-one years in power, the Nationalist government seemed to be showing no signs of impaired vigour, no loss of confidence, and no erosion of its predominating ideology. It had confounded the predictions of those who had believed that a regime of this kind could not continue in a world which professed opinions that conflicted, on one side or the other, with the basic premise of Afrikanerdom. The world might disapprove, but South Africa continued to exist and to prosper.

Its stability of government contrasted sharply with the confusion and chaos to be found elsewhere on the African continent. It was clear that the ordinary processes of white politics would not produce an alternative government, and that the country as a sovereign state was immune to anything but attack from a major power. There was no indication that any major power, however much it might disapprove of the official ideology of South Africa, was prepared to intervene by force. The episode of the Congo had provided one example of the cost of intervention, and it seemed certain that, after the prolonged agony in Vietnam, the Americans were not disposed for further adventures. Those who had talked hopefully about the power of the United Nations to coerce South Africa had overlooked the reality that the power of the United Nations was that of its principal members, and that these had preoccupations of their own nearer home. The whole course of the 1960s had led to a growing disenchantment with Africa on the part of most major powers. Furthermore, as the United States became torn by racial conflict, the problems confronting the formation of a multi-racial society began to seem more pressing and complex than had hitherto been imagined.

Indeed, it could be said, at the end of 1969, that the main threat to the Nationalist Government came, not from 'world opinion' and the indefinite threat of action

Left: Dr Verwoerd with Chief Jonathan of Lesotho, shortly before the former's assassination — evidence of a new Nationalist determination to cultivate friends in black African states

from outside, nor from African states, nor from the white opposition groups, but from its own right wing. In 1969 the right wing of the National Party broke away, to form its own party, claiming that it, and not Vorster, represented the true 'spirit of the *volk*'. It was led by Dr Albert Hertzog, son of the former Prime Minister. The break was the logical sequence to the ideological dispute between *verligtes* and *verkramptes*; the underlying quarrel turned on the whole future relationship towards new African states, and by implication towards the internal policy of apartheid, with its eventual promise of some form of self-determination for the African homelands. It could seem that Vorster was threatened in the 1960s as Botha had been threatened in 1912, and Hertzog had been threatened after 1934. The essential difference was that in the 1960s the question at issue was the eventual attitude to the African population, whereas in the earlier conflicts it had turned on the place of the South African English.

It might seem that the future of South Africa would depend on the price which men and women, on either side of the colour line, would be prepared to pay for order. The first African resistance movements had been broken, at a high cost to their leaders. It remains to be seen how seriously their successors, either within the country, or in training as 'liberatory forces' or 'terrorists' outside, will be prepared to risk their liberty or their lives in what might seem a forlorn hope. It is a disquieting thought, to those raised in the tradition of European liberalism, that political liberty is by no means always desired, and that the classic freedoms of 18th-century enlightenment are not necessarily in themselves conditions of survival or affluence. White South Africans have come to accept, apathetically or with enthusiasm, a high degree of government control over their own activities. Many of them consider it not too high a price for the security which they enjoy. The non-whites have recognised that they can expect no significant help from outside. Most of them have come to accept the fact of apartheid, and to live with it. There are no significant signs that the 'winds of change' will blow south of the Limpopo River for a very long time.

Right: A military parade in Pretoria marks the fifth anniversary of the republic. South Africa could afford to be unimpressed by the hostile gestures of her northern neighbours

Chronology of Events

1652	Jan van Riebeeck lands at the Cape of Good Hope
1689	Huguenot settlers arrive from Holland
1795	The Cape of Good Hope is captured by the British
1803	Treaty of Amiens. The Cape is restored to the Dutch
1806	The Cape is recaptured by the British
1815	The Boers rebel at Slagters Nek
1820	4,000 British colonists arrive in South Africa
1834	Slavery is abolished throughout the British Empire
1835	The Great Trek begins
1838	The Boers defeat the Zulus at Blood River
1842	British authority is established in Natal
1848	The British annex Orange and Vaal River territories
1852	At the Sand River Convention Britain recognises the independence of the Transvaal
1867	Diamonds are discovered at Hopetown near Kimberley
1871	The diamond territory is annexed by the British
1877	The Transvaal is annexed by the British
1879	The Zulu War breaks out
1881	The Convention of Pretoria grants independence to the Transvaal
1883	Kruger becomes President of the Transvaal
1886	Gold is discovered on the Witwatersrand

1890	Cecil Rhodes becomes Prime Minister of the Cape Colony
1893	Gandhi arrives in South Africa
1895	The Jameson Raid fails to overthrow Kruger's republic
1899	The Boer War begins
1902	The Treaty of Vereeniging establishes British rule
1907	Louis Botha becomes Prime Minister in the Transvaal Gandhi leads a civil rights protest campaign
1909	Union of South Africa and Botha becomes Prime Minister
1912	The South African Native National Congress is formed
1918	The *Broederbond* (Afrikaner secret society) is formed
1919	Jan Christiaan Smuts becomes Prime Minister
1922	The Rand Revolt by white miners who feel threatened by black labour
1922	Urban residential segregation is enforced by law
1924	Hertzog becomes Prime Minister
1932	Hertzog abandons the gold standard
1933	Hertzog and Smuts form a coalition government
1934	Daniel Malan founds the National Party
1939	With Smuts as Prime Minister, South Africa enters the Second World War
1946	India severs trade relations with South Africa
1948	Daniel Malan defeats Smuts to become Prime Minister at the head of the Nationalist and Afrikaner Parties

1950	Hendrik Verwoerd becomes Minister of Native Affairs
1951	The Bantu Authorities Act provokes African hostility
1953	The government makes protest movements illegal
1954	Johannes Strijdom becomes Prime Minister
1955	The Freedom Charter voices non-white protests
1956	60,000 Coloured voters are removed from the electoral roll in Cape Province, and non-whites are ordered to vacate their homes in sections of Johannesburg
1958	Hendrik Verwoerd becomes Prime Minister
1959	The Promotion of Bantu Self-Government Act is passed
1960	Police fire on an unarmed crowd in the Sharpeville riot
1961	South Africa becomes a republic
1966	Verwoerd is assassinated and Vorster becomes Prime Minister

Top right: *Jan van Riebeeck, founder of South Africa (left); half-caste Hottentot (centre); early view of Cape Town (right).*
Middle: *Cecil Rhodes's favourite photograph of himself (left); British Boer War propaganda – the Boers turn down the angel of peace (centre); war correspondents in Mafeking (right).*
Bottom: *Jan Smuts (left); poster issued during the campaign to boycott South African goods (centre); cartoon by Low entitled 'Evolution' – a comment on the questionable nature of South Africa's 'forward-looking' policies*

INSTITUTE

FOR TEACHING THE
COLOURED PEOPLES THE BLESSINGS
OF UNCIVILIZATION

PRIMITIVE
PRE-MALAN
MAN

EARLY
MALAN
MAN

LATER
MALAN
MAN

STILL LATER
MALAN
MAN

NEOCOSMIC
OOZE

boycott
apartheid

Index of main people, places, and events

Author's suggestions for further reading

The best brief analysis of South Africa is L.Marquard's *The Peoples and Policies of South Africa* (Oxford University Press 1962); the author is an Afrikaner liberal. It may be supplemented by C.W.de Kiewiet's *A History of South Africa: Social and Economic* (Oxford University Press 1966).

The period of the Boer War and its aftermath is covered by *The Fall of Kruger's Republic* by J.S.Marais (Oxford University Press 1961), *British Supremacy in South Africa 1899-1907* by G.H.Le May (Oxford University Press 1965), and *The Unification of South Africa 1902-10* by L.M.Thompson (Oxford University Press 1960).

Sir Keith Hancock's two-volume biography of General Smuts— *The Sanguine Years* and *The Fields of Force* (Cambridge University Press, Vol. I 1962, Vol. II 1968)—is indispensable for the period 1895-1950. *The South African Opposition 1939-1945* by M.Roberts and A.E.G. Trollip (Longmans 1947) is a brilliant analysis of the Nationalist movements during the Second World War.

The first years of Nationalist government are analysed in depth by G.Carter in *The Politics of Inequality* (Thames and Hudson 1958). Non-white politics are analysed by E.Roux (from the far Left) in *Time Longer Than Rope* (University of Wisconsin Press 1968) and by J.Ngubane in *An African Explains Apartheid* (Pall Mall Press 1963). The Nationalist point of view is explained in *Apartheid* by N.J. Rhoodie and H.J.Venter (University of Pretoria 1960).

Library of the 20th Century will include the following titles:

Russia in Revolt
David Floyd
The Second Reich
Harold Kurtz
The Anarchists
Roderick Kedward
Suffragettes International
Trevor Lloyd
War by Time-Table
A.J.P.Taylor
Death of a Generation
Alistair Horne
Suicide of the Empires
Alan Clark
Twilight of the Habsburgs
Z.A.B.Zeman
Early Aviation
Sir Robert Saundby
Birth of the Movies
D.J.Wenden
America Comes of Age
A.E.Campbell
Lenin's Russia
G.Katkov
The Weimar Republic
Sefton Delmer
Out of the Lion's Paw
Constantine Fitzgibbon
Japan: The Years of Triumph
Louis Allen
Communism Takes China
C.P.FitzGerald
Black and White in South Africa
G.H. Le May
Woodrow Wilson
R.H.Ferrell
France 1918-34
W.Knapp
France 1934-40
A.N.Wahl
Mussolini's Italy
Geoffrey Warner
The Little Dictators
A.Polonsky
Viva Zapata
L.Bethell
The World Depression
Malcolm Falkus
Stalin's Russia
A.Nove
The Brutal Reich
Donald Watt
The Spanish Civil War
Raymond Carr
Munich: Czech Tragedy
K.G.Robbins

Godfrey Le May is Fellow and Tutor in Politics at Worcester College, Oxford. He was, for a time, a journalist on the Johannesburg *Star* and, during the war, he was assistant editor of *The Sudan Star* of Khartoum. He was educated at the Rhodes University College and Worcester College. After holding a lectureship at Balliol College, Oxford, he returned to South Africa as the first Professor of Political Studies in the University of the Witwatersrand, a chair which he held for 14 years. He has published *British Supremacy in South Africa, 1899-1907*, in addition to a collection of documents on British government, and many articles.

J.M.Roberts, General Editor of the *Macdonald Library of the 20th Century*, is Fellow and Tutor in Modern History at Merton College, Oxford. He was General Editor of Purnell's *History of the 20th Century*, is Joint-Editor of the *English Historical Review*, and author of *Europe 1880-1945* in the Longman's History of Europe. He has been English Editor of the Larousse Encyclopedia of Modern History, has reviewed for *The Observer, New Statesman* and *Spectator,* and given talks on the BBC.

Library of the 20th Century

Editor: Jonathan Martin
Executive Editor: Richard Johnson
Designed by: Brian Mayers/ Germano Facetti
Design: HCB Designs
Research: John Deakin

Pictures selected from the following sources:

African National Congress 70 71 80
Anti-Apartheid Movement 90 112
L'Assiette au Beurre 41
Associated Press 102 105 118 121
Ian Berry/Magnum 114
Black Star 82 86 87 89
Camera Press 94 116 117
Ernest Cole/Magnum 92 96 108
Daily Mail 107
Patrick Eagar 98
Elliott and Fry Ltd 42
Foreign Office Library 15 20
Imperial War Museum 40 68 71 74 76
Keystone Press Agency 52 72 84 89 105 110
Magnum 116
Mansell Collection 26 43
National Maritime Museum on loan from the Admiralty 4
National Army Museum 18
Popperfoto 36 38 39 44 117
Radio Times Hulton 12 24 31 33 42 43 54 58
Snark International 42 47
John Seymour 116
United Press International 115
U.S.P.G. 99